**A TRUE STORY FROM
A REAL FAKE**

LITTLE
BOY BLUE

THE CON THEY NEVER
CAUGHT

DEAN COOK

First published in Great Britain in 2025

Editing, typesetting and publishing by UK Book Publishing.

www.ukbookpublishing.com

ISBN: 978-1-918077-48-3

I would like to dedicate this book to my parents.

*To my mother, who managed to beat
the system in her own way by going
decades without becoming a slave to it.*

*And also, to my father. You showed me that
you can work hard, put in all the hours
under the sun – and you still get fucked.*

Without you both I would not be who I am today.

Acknowledgments

To 'Del', my partner in crime on the Treasure Hoard Con, without you this book wouldn't have even got off the ground. You're an inspiration and the Godfather of the hustle. Thanks, mate.

To Matt and Fran, my little bookworms. Thank you for the pointers and direction with the synopsis.

To the town's library staff. Thank you for your input and letting me use your computers and printer for the seemingly endless hard copies and small adaptations throughout.

To the whole team at Roots for their help with the book cover, thank you for your patience and great work, we got there in the end.

Acknowledgments

Contents

Prologue

I think it's about time to tell you my story, well, my story so far at least. The bit some of you may be interested in. Before we start, I would just like to point out that I am retired. Now that I have entered my forties the rush of dopamine my brain once received from being 'up to no good' has run its course. It's time to call it a day, hang up the gloves and walk away. I have somehow managed to get this far without ever being caught and I intend to keep it that way. So, for any PC plods, budding detectives or investigation teams reading: I am no longer a threat to society (to be honest I don't think I ever really was), no longer active and no longer benefiting financially through unlawful means. I am a retired scam artist, fraudster, con and hustler, but I was never a scoundrel. I have never scammed any poor old ladies out of their pension money nor have I conned poor people out of large sums of their hard-earned money. For the most part my schemes involved large businesses, corporations and people with money to burn. Any monies I did make have been re-distributed and any possessions I have now have been acquired legitimately, legally and above board.

I am writing this book mainly for two reasons. The first one is for you, to give you an entertaining read by detailing some of the shenanigans I got up to in the past. And the second is for me, to try and find out why I got up to so many antics? Why didn't I just get a normal 9-5 like most of the others in my family and people I know? What drives the conman and what does he fulfil by carrying out his scams? Well, let's find out…

CHAPTER 1

Con Before the Storm

The Beginning

Con Artist – *A person who cheats or tricks others by persuading them to believe something that is not true.*

Hustler – *a person adept at aggressive selling or illicit dealing.*

(The Oxford Dictionary)

'Con' is short for confidence. In order to obtain money or valuable items from a certain person or party you must first build up a level of trust. It's this trust that can then be used to make financial gains through manipulation and exploitation. I haven't always been a devious little shit bag. So where did it all begin?

(in fast forward)
I was born 24 miles north-west of London, England, in early March 1983. My mother and I first lived with my grandparents in their maisonette until we were moved to

a 'halfway house' – basically a place you called home until you were moved somewhere more permanent. We weren't at the halfway house very long before settling down in a block of flats in Grovehill – a housing development set up in the late 60s and early 70s to house the working classes spilling out from London. This is the place where my memories started life at four years of age, the very first one being my mother teaching me to ride my bike without stabilisers for the first time. I remember it, clear as a bell. It was a bright, sunny day and I was riding up a pavement towards a brick wall that was waist high. I remember looking back, expecting to see my mother behind me but she wasn't there. She had let go some distance back and to my amazement I was doing it all by myself. It's funny how your brain does that, just wakes up one day and starts recalling things. I don't remember anything before that day, but I remember a lot of what came after. My second memory is again, outside the flat, just a few feet away from where I was riding my bike. This time I was on my dad's lap in the front seat of his car. It was a 1961 Ford Zephyr with a 2.3 litre straight six, blood red with a white roof – a beautiful car, which is no doubt where my love for classic cars was born. He was teaching me to drive, well, to steer anyway. As far as I was concerned, I was driving that beast – and it was awesome.

My third memory is with our old neighbour, a horrible woman, who used to 'look after' me while my mum and dad were away. She had two daughters, both had long blonde hair that went right down to their backsides. We would play out front until it was time to come in for something to eat. One day she slammed a plate of toast onto the table in front of me and snarled through gritted teeth 'don't tell your dad that I don't give you anything!'. Now, this isn't much to write home about, but I remember in particular the contrast between how she spoke to her daughters and how she spoke to me. To her daughters she was sweet, loving and gentle. But to me, she was feral, nasty and vicious, especially towards a four-year-old boy.

Years later my mother would tell me that my father was having an affair with her at the time – which I guess could explain it. But what the fuck did I do wrong? She ended up in prison years later for stealing. Good riddance to the bitch.

My fourth and final memory, is from inside the flat. Every week we had a video rental guy that would come around with a bag of VHS tapes. Every week he came, and every week I would ask to have the same film, which was a cartoon. He would show me what else he had in his bag, and my mum would ask me if I wanted to pick something different. But every week I would choose the same. Anyway, one particular week we had a knock at the door. It was a bailiff coming round to collect a debt, which my mum didn't have the money to pay. He said he was going to take the television, so my mother pointed him towards me, who was sat in front of the television at the time. The bailiff took pity; he gave her another week – and left me to continue watching my cartoon.

And that's it from the flat. Apart from a few flashbacks of other bits and pieces I don't remember much else. We would soon move house to Ritcroft Close. Ritcroft was a proper house, it had a front and back garden, a big green out the front to play on, and plenty of kids to play with. I started school at Redding's Primary which was only walking distance away. My class was made up of mainly Asian kids from Pakistan, a few white, with the token black kid. Jamille, Gary and Richard, one from every ethnic group, were my friends. At Ritcroft I made friends with two siblings, a brother and a sister who were two years apart. They lived around the corner from me. We would pretend to be the Rice Krispie kids from the cereal box: Snap, Crackle & Pop. We'd wear our capes and fly around the street while the other older kids on the estate played football on the green. I wanted to play football with them to begin with; they let me play on a few occasions but more often than not I was bullied off the pitch and pushed out of play. For such a small boy I still held my own, it was on this pitch that I had my first ever fight with an older boy. He'd wrestled me to the ground one day and started punching me in the face. I managed to pull him towards me and turn us both around; so, I was on top and could get the upper-hand. I remember my mum leaning out of the upstairs window screaming for me to 'fucking hit him', which I did. I beat the shit out of that kid. The others eventually dragged me off and I went indoors and burst into tears. It was a combination of all the adrenaline plus the fact that I thought I was in trouble. This wasn't the case at all, my mum met me with joy, congratulated me on my win and told me to stop crying. She said she was going to tell my dad when he got home and that he'd be happy.

For a little while after the older kids let me play football with them but it wouldn't last. Once all the parents were safely inside and out of sight, they would take me and my two friends to the wooded area next to the green. The boy in charge of the pack was 16 and gave the orders while the others watched. We were made to take our clothes off and do things to each other that we had no business doing at such a young age. The sick fucks would make the brother and sister do things to each other while I looked on, then me with the boy, then the girl, and so on. Those poor fuckers. I wonder if they remember that shit to this day. They must do. Siblings as well. Horrible.

They did lots of weird shit come to think about it. One day they decided to befriend me and my little friend, just me and the boy this time. They ushered us into the wooded area again, hidden amongst all the greenery. They didn't make us take our clothes off on this particular day; this time they made us fight. I have a feeling of guilt, even now, for that poor little boy. He didn't want to fight, and wouldn't. I too didn't want to fight, but did – because they told me to. They cheered me on after each punch. I beat the shit out of my friend as well that day, and I don't know why. I didn't even like the other kids, but I wanted to be accepted by them, I guess. Eventually the poor little mite went home sobbing to his mum, who later came round to reprimand me, and so she should have.

We used to have an ice cream van that would come around when the sun was out. One day I snuck out my savings tin that was full of pennies. I bought every kid on the street a screwball then snuck the tin back inside. I remember getting a good telling off for that but it was worth it. I was popular for a moment and the older kids left me alone that day. But that, too, wouldn't last.

Not long after that we had a big water fight on the green. For some reason one of the older girls decided to up the ante and took it upon herself to go inside and boil a kettle (this was the same girl that I'd had my first 'sexual' encounter with at a sleepover some time previously – I say sexual encounter, I was only five so it was only simulation, she was showing me what her parents did to each other in their bedroom – and she knew far too much).

I remember screaming as she poured the boiled water over me. I clawed my back trying to make it go away. One of the older boys, the head honcho of the woods, picked me up to take me in to my dad so he could be the hero. Although my skin was burning, I remember not wanting him to touch me. I didn't like the big hero charade or my dad thanking him for bringing me home. Luckily my dad's friend was over visiting our house. He was in the territorial army so knew to put me straight into the cold shower to try and neutralise the burn. I was taken straight to the burns unit at the hospital and bandaged from head-to-toe and came out looking like a mummy. My dad's friend Anthony is the reason I am not covered in scars today.

And that was that, we moved away from all that shit and came to the south-west of England, a fresh start, at the age of six. It was after this move that I would start to experience what I have come to know as anxiety. I was only six and had already moved from my grandparents to the halfway house, from the halfway house to the flat, from the flat to the house at Ritcroft, then from there to the new house in Devon. In that time, I had been treated badly by my father's mistress, been sexually abused by the older kids on the estate, put in hospital twice through being burned, had run ins with an inappropriate babysitter, taught how the adults have sex and had already been in several fights.

In Devon we were having tests in school and it was the first time I felt like I was being judged – something I had never been through before. I used to cry in school because of the pressure. It shouldn't have mattered; it was as if my whole life depended on the results of these Maths and spelling tests. I think I was just concentrating all my fears, stress and worry on these tests alone.

Primary school in the South-West went well. I started to make friends and became best buddies with my next-door neighbour Karl, who is still my best buddy today. I got a girlfriend – Natalie – who remained my girlfriend right up until secondary school when we were separated (I have recently found out that Natalie drowned in a bath not long ago – such a shame. She was a sweet and lovely kid; we hooked up briefly years later and had a fling. We would talk of those long summer days at school, playing kiss chase in the playground and rounders out on the field – her in her red and white summer dresses and me in my little grey shorts and yellow polo shirt. Happy times.

Secondary school in Devon was good. I was only there for a couple of years before my mother decided she wanted another fresh start. Before long we were packed up again and on our way to Leighton Buzzard, not too far from where we had started out – another shit hole. I changed schools, this time I had to go to a middle school and make friends again. I found it hard but started to settle, I had made a friend and met a girl, Lil. She lived at 72 Grasmere Way. She was tall, slim but not skinny – with a figure that would fill out into the perfect hourglass. She had long, wavy blonde hair and deep blue eyes that you could dive right into. Intelligent, sweet and polite but definitely not a pushover – she was strong, like a lioness but with the hint of an English rose – gorgeous in every possible way.

We met at an army cadet detachment and would walk home together. She was 16, two years older than me and let me know not long after we met that she liked me. I had wanted to ask her out but didn't because my friend Ben also had the hots for her. In the end, on one of our walks home she said, 'are you going to ask me out or not?', so I did and we became boyfriend and girlfriend.

I would see Lil at school. I still remember the way she glided through the school corridor, head up, confident, with her best friend Laura. Sometimes she would see me and other times she wouldn't. We would meet up every day during break times and again after school. She'd come over to my house and I would go over to hers. When we were at her house, she would sing to me over a tape recording that she had of piano music. I would sit at the end of her bed as she sat in front of her mirror at her make-up stand.

She gave me a tape of her singing once for Valentine's Day; I kept it for years along with her love letters but my ex discovered them and threw them away in jealousy – along with the songs and soppy poems I had written about her. When she came to mine, I would walk her home after. And when it was cold she would give me her coat to wear on my way back home. It was a red and yellow jacket made from shell-suit material and it just about fit me – although a little too short in the arms. I can still remember her perfume on the jacket.

We would go ice-skating together and meet up with my friend Ben and Laura and play tennis. Boys versus girls then me and Lil versus the other two. One day we met up and Ben came along. We were sat in a shelter and Ben got pissed off because he felt like he was being left out of the conversation so went home. Lil called Ben the gentleman and me the smooth guy. She said he was the kind that would open a door for her whereas I'd run straight through it. Somehow Lil and I ended up in the bushes. It's probably not the most romantic but it was, for sure, the most erotic moment I had ever had up until that point. We were there for a long time until it got dark and were eventually picked up by our dads – who were not best pleased. We sat in the back seat of the car, holding hands in silence and smiling. Lil told me she wanted her first time to be romantic, not in a bush, and she wanted it to happen in a hotel – unfortunately funds I did not have at 14.

It was at 13/14 that I started to rebel. My body was changing, my voice broke and I started to grow upwards, fast. In an effort to show that we had more money at Leighton Buzzard my parents bought me my first pair of genuine Reebok trainers (because we would soon be visiting Devon again and my mum didn't want me hassling them to go back home). I remember being in the shop with her and she said I had the choice of a bigger, cheaper brand pair or a smaller pair that were the Reeboks (they were only a size six and a half). I chose the pair that were too small for me because I was desperate to have them. They hurt my feet which was a small price to pay in the short term but would cost me eventually because as my feet grew, my toes became crippled with most of them turning inwards. Eventually one foot literally burst out of the trainer. The Reeboks were good while they lasted and I fucking loved them – and my feet are still crippled now.

With my new-found size advantage, I stopped taking shit from anyone that wanted to give it to me and got into dozens of fights in middle school. I had a temper that would erupt when I was being taken advantage of. One day some of the kids followed me and my classmate into the toilets. One of them thought it would be a good idea to smash my head into the taps as I was trying to take a drink. I lost my shit, pushed him into a cubicle and beat the living daylights out of him. His friends didn't do anything, and from then on, I was left alone.

There were other fights but those were mainly to settle the scores of who was where in the rankings of 'hardest kid in school', and in what order. I wasn't the hardest but I definitely wasn't going to be taking any shit from anyone any more.

It was less than a year and my mother wanted to up sticks and move, again. Now it was back down to the South-West. I had to go and break the news to Lil; she wanted us to stay together but my family had insisted that long-distance relationships didn't work so I told her that it was over but to stay in touch.

I remember the day I ended it with her. We were standing outside her mum and dad's house by the front porch where their house telephone was, the same one we would chat on of an evening with the whole 'no, you put the phone down first' carry on. She was crying and we hugged. She said she would come and visit me on the train and I said she could. We said our goodbyes and I walked home, past the train station for the very last time.

I'll never forget that last letter I wrote to Lil – inside I was missing her like mad and I didn't know what love was until she was gone. But I made out in the letter that I wasn't really interested. It broke me inside to write like that to her, but it was a last-ditch effort to get her to move on and forget me, which she did.

It wasn't long until she told me that she had met someone else. 'Ryan' and her were an item, he had proposed to her and they spent the night in a hotel. Game over. I let her be.

I still think about Lil, even now, and I don't think I ever really stopped loving her. It was missing her so much that inspired me to start writing in my mid-teens. She's still with Ryan and married with two kids. I found her on Facebook and every now and then I check in to see any new photos that she has put on. We're not even friends on there but I can still see some pics.

I've always wanted to let her know about that last letter I wrote and that I didn't mean it – and how much I've regretted it ever since. I saw the film Titanic not long after returning to Devon and it reminded me so much of Lil. She was the pistol and I was the poor kid with nothing to offer her.

It was such a long time ago. Maybe some things should be left in the past, plus I still occasionally got to see her in my sleep.

I know she is happy – and that's enough.

Veni, Vidi, Vici.

And that's it, back down to sunny Devon with my old classmates. When I left, I was short, childlike with a squeaky voice; then when I came back, I was towering above everyone. The rebellion continued and I became a little shit. I was getting into fights on a weekly basis and was a nightmare for the teachers. I thought I was being cool and really just didn't give a fuck.

My friend Lewis and I broke into the school canteen after hours and stole as many chocolate bars that we could fit into two rucksacks. The next day I began my first hustle and started selling them in school.

My brother and I didn't have a lot growing up, but our clothes were clean and we were just about fed. Thankfully we had free school dinners for a short while in primary school. The bastard dinner ladies would make the poor kids on welfare line up separately to the paying kids – a nice social divide. When that ended it was shocking school lunches for the next ten years consisting of slimy pickle sandwiches, just pickle and no cheese, a bag of crisps –which really was a bag of air because they came from the cheap shop, and a Penguin biscuit.

To this day I am traumatised by fucking pickle, for my brother it's lettuce – for the same reason as me. And Penguins, if I never see another bastard Penguin again it'll still be too soon. I never understood the slimy pickle sandwich deal. I would have accepted that it was because it was all the food we had, but it wasn't what my parents ate. My mum kept her own cheese in the top of the fridge and my dad ate out because he was away. As a kid I got used to being hungry at school and would be jealous of my friends packed lunch boxes, eyeing up what their mothers had packed for them and wishing that I'd had the same. My mother always seemed to find the money for her expensive tailor-made cigarettes, her magazines and to get her hair done whenever she wanted it doing.

I remember in PSE (personal social education), we had to do a class exercise on the amount of money we got. We had to write down a list of what we got each week, pocket money, what was spent on us, etc. The whole point of the exercise was to come to the realisation that we were more fortunate than we originally thought we were – and to become aware of how much our parents really did for us. All the kids in the class were writing down what they got each week but I was struggling to come up with things to put onto paper. I started to put down that I was fed, clothed and had a roof over my head, but was told to cross it out by the teacher and to write just about money. She thought I was being belligerent when I told her that I had nothing to write down because we were poor.

School can be a cruel place if you're not kitted out in named brands. It was all Nike, Adidas, Puma, Reebok and Kickers then. If you weren't wearing any of that, you were a scrub. My mum had bought me some white trainers from the market; they lit up when the soles touched the ground. One of the trainers was a bit iffy so I had to stamp my foot down in order for it to work. I loved them, but I knew the other kids wouldn't. In an effort to fit in I practised drawing the Nike tick on paper until I got it perfect. Once I was happy with my design, I got a permanent marker and drew the tick onto my trainers. It worked. One of the other kids commented that I had on the new 'Nike Lights' and that he liked them. That was it, it was like a lightbulb came on in my mind – and my art in deception and fraud was born.

CHAPTER 2

Every King and Queen

The Banknote Con

I hardly went to school that final year, most of it was spent playing truant, smoking down the alleyway near school, or over at a friend's house, drinking. One day we raided my friend Lewis' parents' drinks cabinet. We took two girls back with us and got smashed at lunchtime. One of the girls had drunk so much that she passed out and needed the paramedics. They pumped her stomach at the hospital and it turned out she was okay.

I saw her years later on a bus one day and she was spouting off about God and everything the good lord had done for us. Maybe our mad lunchtime had turned her to religion.

Our school canteen shenanigans had landed me in a cell. I knew the police were coming because Lewis had already had a visit from the boys in blue. I had to be questioned with my parents being that I was still a minor. I remember my mum putting all the airs and graces on in front of the police – with my dad doing the complete opposite. He hated them with a passion, treated them with contempt, and he let them know it. I denied everything and as luck would have it, I didn't leave any fingerprints.

They knew it was me but couldn't prove anything. All they knew for sure was that I was there because I had been grassed up, so I went away with the maximum they could charge me with, which was a caution for aiding and abetting.

We quickly outgrew the canteen lark and sought the next buzz. Before long we were breaking into other schools for the gym and sports equipment and selling whatever we could fit into our rucksacks and carry back with us.

Karl and I broke into a train once; there wasn't much in it, but we took anything that we could sell on. My friend Shane went back for a second time but got caught red-handed, in the cash office.

By now I was smoking weed. I'd been to Spain and brought back a pipe for my friend Karl from the market – it came in three parts that you could put together. We knew a guy we called the Mexican and he asked us if we were going to spend all day looking at it or were we going to smoke it. Karl went first, took a lungful then passed it to me. I copied what he did, trying my hardest not to look like a complete novice and gave it my best shot, took my very own lungful and managed to complete the task without coughing. This was to be my first day at the school of cannabis – where I would become top of my class for the next five years.

We quickly worked out that instead of spending £10 for an 8th of an ounce of hashish, if we bought the whole ounce for £60 then we could make some smoke for us and have £10 left over. So that's what we did, just an ounce each to begin with. Then once that ounce was sold get another, and another, and so on. Before long, it was an ounce of amphetamine, then 100 ecstasy pills, then 200, then 500. I was the world's worst drug dealer – mainly because I had them all. The first rule in 'how to become a successful drug dealer' is to not get high on your own supply. The trouble I found is I got so high I couldn't remember who the fuck I'd sold to and who owed me money. I would take a bunch of ecstasy tablets, give a load out when I was all loved up and best friends with everyone, then when it was time to collect – everyone seemed to have a bad case of memory loss, me included.

We'd get high on amphetamine and go out and steal petrol, raid the washing lines on campsites for the designer clothes and steal alloy wheels to order.

Karl and I needed to get to Cheltenham once and we needed a lot of fuel to get there, so, we raided the contents of a coach's fuel tank. Not long after we had four jerry cans full to the brim of red diesel and we were off up the motorway. That very car we drove up in, a red Peugeot 405, got clamped once we were there – with a £50 release charge. We were heading to the cinema where there were lots of jackets hanging on the backs of chairs so luckily, we came away with a wallet that was loaded and the fee was paid.

Drug dealing and thievery wasn't for me but I needed a way of making money – that didn't require going out and working in factories – as that was the only unskilled work around at the time.

I didn't know what I wanted to be when I grew up, I was thinking about the army but I was still too young, so I enrolled in college on a public services course – a course designed to gear you up for the army, NHS, police force, ambulance and fire service. In the meantime, I had met a girl, Amy, very attractive and way above me in social standing. Her parents were rich compared to mine and I always felt out of my depth in their presence. They lived in a nice street; they were a two-car family and had two bathrooms. Amy had her own room with all the latest gadgets, a brand-new state of the art computer and the best printer that money could buy at the turn of the millennium. I'd been taught in college how to use a computer; at first, I didn't even know how to switch one on as I'd never used one before – but I'd soon learn.

I'd been thinking about the whole concept of money for a while. Everyone chasing it, beg, stealing and borrowing it. People spending their whole lives working for it, when all it really is, is bits of paper with the queen's head on – tokens to get stuff. It got me wondering if there was a way in which I could get some.

The whole point of using money in the first place is to simplify transactions. Way back when, we used to trade goods, swap, and barter. Money is a made-up thing which gives us a belief that you can store value, it's only valuable because we believe it is – the same as gold and diamonds. Gold is just a yellow metal that comes from the ground, much the same as other metals – it just looks nice when polished and made into jewellery. There's an argument that there's only so much of it, which makes it rare, i.e. valuable, but it's just a metal extracted from the ground. The same with diamonds, they are not rare, nowhere near as rare as you think they are. So, why is the diamond trade a multi-billion-pound industry? It's because you think they are rare, that's why. You have been taught that they are expensive, beautiful and hard to come by – it's all bullshit, a con, a magic trick – but more on that later.

The use of money facilitates the exchange of goods and is a way of measuring the value of these goods. So why can't we just print more of it? Governments could do this, the problem being it would lead to hyperinflation and currency devaluation. The less there is of something, the more it is 'worth'. Currency is tied to the services and goods that it can buy – by printing more of it would decrease its purchasing power. That didn't stop many of us from trying anyway.

Counterfeit money has been around for as long as money has existed. Whether it be notes or coins, people have always tried to replicate it in order to obtain things that they want, without having to really 'earn' it. I say 'earn', what I really mean is to slave for it, well – the majority of people anyway.

This was to be my first real scam and the smallest in comparison to the rest – but they had to start somewhere. From juvenile beginnings to worldwide carnage by the end. This was just a drop in the ocean – and rivers run deep.

I said I'd been thinking about money for a while, I mean, it's just paper and ink, right? How hard could it be? I started experimenting with all the notes that good old Blighty had to offer in the very early 2000s – 5s, 10s, 20s & 50s. I scanned all the notes onto the computer. It was the best software that money could buy at the time but they didn't look good. The 5s were okay but they were of such low denomination that it wasn't worth it. The 10s were terrible – the orange colour was out by a country mile and the 20s weren't much better. The 50s looked good but they were the complete opposite to the 5s – too high of a denomination and people would be all over them like rash.

At the time I had got myself a job working in an Irish bar in town – the landlord was a dick but it was the busiest bar in town. I had lied at my job interview and put on my CV that I'd had two previous bar jobs. I told them that I had experience pulling pints, changing barrels and making cocktails – all bullshit, but I figured out I could wing it – which I did. After a couple of shoddy pints, I had worked it out – being that I was pouring my dad his beers since I was a kid, tilting the glass then altering the angle as the beer reached the top. I put off changing the barrels for as long as I could, then eventually got one of the bar girls to show me. I made out the previous bar I had worked in had slightly different apparatus – more bullshit but it worked.

I had a scam going over the bar, I would take the pissed punters' orders and skim off the top. If the round came to £30, I would take a £10 note for myself, if it was £20 then I would take £5. The customer wouldn't be getting ripped off, it's just that a certain percentage of it wouldn't make its way to the till. I would get a friend to come with me for a free night's drinking, they would pay whatever the round came to, and in their change, I would put the money I had just skimmed off the top of all the other orders. They'd pay me with a £10 or £20 note, which I'd put into the till and give back £50 in change. That way I never had to keep a pocket full of notes. It was a simple scam, but very effective and we took a lot – especially at weekends.

It was this bar where the counterfeit money scam went up a notch. In my wages one Friday I received two Scottish £10 notes – those were the days when you were paid in cash in a small brown envelope. It was the first time I had seen Scottish money and it didn't look real – but I was assured it was legal tender and people had to accept them. They had the watermarks and the broken foil lines but the ink looked dull and the paper seemed to be thin. I uploaded them to the computer and scanned off a few sheets. The ink looked great but the paper was too thick. Plus, I didn't have a watermark and there were no foiled lines.

I visited an art shop where they had a vast paper supply, all different shades of colours and thicknesses. I thumbed through what they had, feeling the paper between my fingers and rubbing the edges. I bought what looked and felt right and went home to try again. I printed off a few more sheets and again, they looked good but they still didn't feel right. I noticed that if I rolled the paper through my fingers, it would stretch the fibres and then felt perfect. I experimented with tin foil and glue to make the broken foil lines but it was too much work, took too long, and the glue affected the paper.

I got around the watermark by cutting the note in half along where the water mark should be, then glued the two sheets back together. This worked great because when you lifted the note up to the light you could see a thicker line where the light couldn't shine through as well as it did with a single sheet. I made a bunch with the water mark and a bunch without. I would put them in the tumble dryer with some items of clothing, eventually the notes would be crinkled and screwed up en masse. I then stained them with tea to give them an aged look and they came out great.

I handed out a few to my friends and family and told them I had got them in my wages and asked if they'd ever seen Scottish money before. It worked and nobody told me they were fake, not even the ones without the watermark, so I figured I didn't even need to do that in future. Now to see if they'd work in the real world.

The first try was in a taxi on a night out. It was dark but the taxi driver still had his internal light on in the cab. I said with confidence that I'd got them in my wages – which was kind of true so I believed it. I've come to learn that being a convincing confidence trickster is all about believing your own bullshit. Once you have mastered that then it's all downhill from then on. The taxi driver took the money and didn't say a thing, told me to have a good night and drove off into the distance. I felt bad for a second then reassured myself that he'd still be on the same money; it would just be the company that is ten pound shy that week when handing their weekly take into the bank.

I had done it, pulled it off and was on my way. Next it was the clubs, pubs and anyone who was happy to take this 'legal tender'. My friends and I had many a night out, as much as we could drink, free taxis and free clubs. Well, it wasn't free, because I was paying.

This worked a treat for a while but it wasn't to last very long. Eventually the different establishments in my hometown stopped accepting Scottish money, they even put a sign out the front of my local off-licence which read: 'NO LONGER ACCEPTING SCOTTISH BANKNOTES'. My plan was foiled – but it was fun while it lasted. It wasn't the biggest of schemes, but it was a start – now onto the next.

CHAPTER 3

Pulled A Flanker

The Pawn Shop Con

B y now I was 18, just finishing College where I'd been, or hardly been for the last two years. I spent most of my time bunking off and getting stoned with my friends. Dreams of the army had faded into the distance and I already had sights on other things. As part of our course, we had to do work experience in our chosen field – ideally something to do with sports or one of the public services. My college friends spent time with the police force, the NHS or the fire service. I had got myself a placement at the local primary school taking PE lessons with the kids. It was brilliant and I nailed it. I felt out of place in the teacher's rec room as I drank their tea and ate their biscuits trying to fit in. They would ask me what I got up to in my spare time. I figured telling them I spent most nights in a car park getting wasted with Karl and Nick was probably not the general chitchat they wanted to hear so I dialled it down, made up some camouflage vanilla bullshit and blagged my way through it.

I loved my time at the school. For the first day I shadowed the PE teacher, then I was allowed to take my own lessons. They let me make my own lesson plans and use all of their equipment. The lessons went well and the kids had a great time. I was invited to work as a teaching assistant in the general classroom which I did alongside the PE lessons until my time was up. We would have story time where the little ankle biters would sit down, all looking up at you wide-eyed, as you told some tales – usually involving treasure, dragons or magic. I would emphasise certain parts of the story and keep them glued – barely containing their excitement. We would make costumes for the school play – The Little Red Riding Hood. Most of the kids had to dress up as wolves so I made them head bands with a wolf head template for each side that they could colour in before being stapled together at the front and sides. I went to the play and the kids did a brilliant job. They even gave me a mention at the end, thanking me for my input. The school wrote me a letter of commendation to take with me to wherever I wanted to apply to after – a nice gesture and something that I have kept. I made my mind up from my time with the kids that I wanted to be a teacher.

My girlfriend and I both applied to university. I wanted to go on the PGCE course, a course that would have got me well on my way into teaching. At first, we had both decided to take a year out to travel but she changed her mind at the last minute – through pressure from her parents. So, we ended up being accepted but onto shit courses – basically whatever they had left in a rush to get us both through clearing. I got given Sociology with Applied Sports Science & Coaching – because of the coaching award I'd received at college, along with the distinction I'd received on one of my college papers – one of them being sociology. I fucking hated it. University was the worst. I was put with the jocks who liked nothing more than masturbating over any game that involved getting a ball of air from one side of a pitch, court or table to the other. I never understood that. I made friends with people from the media and arts department. They had at least half a brain and were quite partial to the odd substance or two.

The only thing that I had in common with the jocks was that there was one sport that I liked – which was boxing. To me, this was a proper sport – a real art.

I had joined the local boxing club when I had just turned 15. I remember reading a book by Harry Carpenter called 'The Hardest Game' – which was a big mistake. In the book he said that if kids hadn't got into boxing by the age of 12 or so then they were likely too old, because by then they were getting interested in girls and going out. I took this as fact, and not thinking about how dated the book was, I believed it and went into boxing; after turning 15 a week prior – already thinking I was too old for the sport.

Training was hard, two laps around town including a run up a fiercely steep hill to finish each lap, then a session of bag work, burpee jumps, sit ups, press ups, rope work, shadow boxing, and sparring. As an extra we'd run up and down the stairs with a medicine ball – harsh training but necessary before stepping into the ring.

After less than six weeks' training, I was put into my first fight, very green, very inexperienced and very keen to please. Normally fighters have at least a year's experience before entering the ring – but they needed to make up the numbers on the fight bill. I was entered onto the bill with a heavier, older and much more experienced lad from the Channel Islands. I did well to survive all rounds but my nose was a mess by the end of it. I got my photo in the local newspaper and my coach said I had showed a lot of heart.

University was the first time I had seen vast amounts of real money in the flesh. We were given a sum every three months which was supposed to go towards books, travel expenses, food and living. I invested mine into copious amounts of ecstasy pills at £1 a go; Mitsubishis, doves, barrels and supermans, a few ounces of weed – which was mainly purple haze at the time – and a few ounces of speed (pink champagne). This was never a real money maker being the terrible drug dealer that I was but the idea was there.

My university was based in Plymouth. It was the first time I'd seen 'proper' shops compared to my small home town – which was like going back in time compared to this place. There were people from all different backgrounds and ethnicities, back home we had one token black kid and that was it for the whole town. In Plymouth they had a vast array of pawn shops and jewellers and I was drawn to them like a magpie. I'd walk past the same ones every day and check out the Rolexes and gold chains and dream of one day being able to own one. The closest I had ever got to seeing a Rolex before was the fakes in Spain at the local market. They were pretty good for their day and would fool some jewellers, at least until they got the back off the watch.

There was one particular pawn shop that I was interested in. It was one of them oldy-woldy ones that had everything – gold, watches, electricals, musical instruments and antiques. They'd buy basically anything if they could steal it from you and put it in their window and sell it for ten times the purchase price. I'd walk past on most days and be drawn to the watches and gold in particular.

From a young age I'd always been kind of obsessed with watches. As a kid I'd kept a biscuit tin full up with them that I'd buy every time I went to a second-hand car boot sale. I'd exchange the straps, take the backs off and try to fix the ones that were broken. I remember once I bought a watch from an old lady, it was in a basket with a bunch of other shrapnel – mainly costume jewellery. I asked her for the price and she said five pence, which was a bargain, but she wasn't going to ask much from the little boy with the innocent smile and blue eyes looking up at her. We were staying at my aunty and uncles at the time – it was my aunty that told me that this watch was a Cartier. It was a combination of stainless steel and solid gold and had a dark blue cabochon crown with a white dial. She said to buy one would cost anywhere between £400-£4000 – depending on how new and which model.

Not long after that it went missing.

In the pawn shop window was a handful of Rolexes. Some stainless steel, some gold and some a mixture of both – all with different dials and bezels. I was obsessed with this shop front the same as I had been about my biscuit tin, and I wanted one of the watches- –but I wasn't going to be able to buy one.

It was our summer off campus for the holidays so Amy and I went out to Spain. We wanted some sun and a break from all of the 'studying', even though there was more time spent getting high than there was reading. I'd been out to Spain quite a few times before as it was a cheap getaway and free digs – given that my grandparents lived there. My usual schedule consisted of plenty of sun, sea and cerveza. I always packed light and took as little clothing as possible in a big case. The reason being I could always bring back as many packs of tobacco as I could squeeze into my bag and physically carry. When I got home, I had a guy who always bought in bulk. In those days customs weren't bothered and everyone was at it. It made enough money to cover my flight and holiday with plenty left over. Back then I could sell a 50-gram pouch of tobacco for £3 and still make a profit. The last time I heard they were reaching £20 and that was a while ago. There was the occasional bottle of booze and box of tailor-made cigarettes, but the bulk of the money came with the rolling tobacco – being that you could squeeze a small fortune into a large case next to a pair of shorts and a few t-shirts.

Years later it would be Valium that cost next to nothing in the Spanish chemists. You could buy them over the counter and at least two boxes from each chemist without raising suspicion. Thirty tablets per box, two boxes from each of the chemists they had in the port

– every few days. At £1 a tablet, when they only cost 70 cents per box – you do the maths. It was good business, but back then it was all about the tobacco – one year I left all of my clothes there – the tobacco was worth more.

Whilst in Spain I would visit the markets. You don't see it so much these days because the authorities are pretty hot on it, but back then there was a glowing trade in counterfeit goods. There were designer watches, wallets, handbags, belts, sunglasses, suitcases, shoes, shirts, sweatshirts, polo shirts, ties – pretty much anything you could think of, they had it – and plenty of it. My main go-to was always the watches. I would scan through what they had on offer – much like the window in the pawn shop. I'd look to see which ones were the most passable. The ones to avoid were the 'busy' watches, the ones that had too much going on, too many sub-dials, buttons and see-through backs.

Anything that was gold or rose gold was another definite no-no. The one I was looking for was the Submariner Date – with the stainless-steel case and bracelet, black bezel and dial with the correct luminous phosphorescent hour markers and hands. It had to be the right weight, have the right shine and feel smooth, not clunky or jingly, and have the sweeping hand of an automatic-movement. The better ones were always more expensive and the guys always had some extras that they'd sell for the right money – ones that were a bit too flashy to be leaving on the tables – as they were easy pickings for the pick-pockets. Once I found the watch that ticked all those boxes I bartered with the man until I got the price I wanted to pay.

I'd been in the pawn shop before on a few occasions. I'd bought a solid gold belcher chain necklace and a pair of gold boxing glove pendants to go on it. I also bought a 9mm semi-automatic Beretta – the old kind that was made from real steel, not the zinc alloy rubbish that they sell in this day and age.

Back then they had masses of ex-service handguns that they needed to sell, so to do it legally they made them into blank firers only. The laws were slack so basically a hole was drilled in the top with the barrels plugged. All the parts needed to still function in order to be able to fire the blanks – a great little gun, which I had to let go for a £400 debt. Years later these would be banned – and rightly so, because everyone was de-plugging the barrels and blocking the holes up to make them fully operational again. At one point every wannabe gangster South of Luton had one – little scallywags.

The woman at the pawn shop was a nice old girl – she had served me two out of the three times I had been there. The other time it was the guy whom I didn't like. He was rude, didn't have much time for me, spoke to me like I was a peasant and was obviously the owner. She was much more pleasant, dressed to impress, like she was trying to pass for a higher class – and wearing strong-smelling perfume. She was going to be the mark. When I spoke to her, I could tell instantly that she was weak, knew a little but not a lot about designer watches and jewellery. She was a jack-of-all trades and he was the master of all regarding expertise for the things that they had for sale.

I'd practised in my dorm room what I was going to do and how I was going to do it. Putting my watch on and slipping it back off again, just with me from my view then in the mirror to see what she would see. I imagined myself in the shop making small talk – turning and looking natural. It made me nervous as I transported myself to the counter, believing the daydream and feeling as if I was there. Once I got it perfect it was time to go.

The heist was to take place at the weekend, when the shop was at its busiest; with lots of people trying things on and with them closing the following day. This would leave the maximum amount of time to pass and only add to the confusion pot. CCTV was still rare then, and the shops that had it only had systems that produced very poor-quality footage that they recorded onto tapes.

I brought my girlfriend along for the ride but she knew nothing of the plan; by her not knowing anything made her actions all the more believable – she wouldn't be acting and everything would be natural. We entered the shop, dressed reasonably smart but not overly. I felt the exact same as I did upon entering a boxing ring. You're almost paralysed with fear until it's time to spring into action – and from somewhere your mind and body knows exactly what to do and when to do it. I was instantly met with the first hurdle – the fuckin guy, Mr rude, the know-it-all of the shop asked if he could help us. 'No mate you can't, fuck off!' I didn't say that but I was thinking it, whilst buzzed; wondering if they knew how I felt inside. 'We're just looking thanks,' I said with a smile, quickly averting my gaze to some of the shiny things he had behind the glass counter. Once he was safely out of earshot and dealing with another customer, I asked the woman if I could have a look at the watches she had in the window. She took down the red velvet window display that had the watches on and I asked to try on the gold Day Date – then put it on my left wrist. I asked Amy what she thought of it, knowing she would hate the gold; thinking it was 'too chavvy' – this was all part of the ploy.

Next, I asked to try the stainless steel Sub Date, which the lady took out and I tried it on, this time on my right wrist – the one that already had the replica on. I asked Amy what she thought of it, which I knew she would have liked and she came back with, 'Yes, I prefer that one', word for word what I was expecting. I turned my back away from the woman and towards Amy, made a remark about the price and that I wasn't sure, then flicked the clasp on the other watch as I'd practised in my room probably 100 times, slipped it over the other and handed it back to the woman. I said I'd think about it but while we were there could we have a look at some of the bracelets. She put the watches back and brought the bracelets out from behind the counter for us to take a closer look at. They were silver and cubic zirconia. Amy said she liked the bangle so I said we'd take it, which we did, along with the watch on my wrist. We left. I didn't look back, never re-visited, spoke about, walked past or even breathed the word 'pawn shop'. Heist over, and a great success. Foolish, ballsy and basic- but it worked.

I got a few hundred for that Rolex, which is nothing in the grand scheme of things, but it was a lot to me.

Not only the money but the experience. Onwards and upwards. I learned a lot from that first switch. Your brain goes 100 miles per hour after you've done it. What about this? What about that? Did I say too much? Did they know? What could I have done better? What I could have done was not perform a switch in a place that I'd already bought gold from before – and a place I'd purchased a firearm from – that was foolish.

I never heard another thing about it. No news bulletin, no house-to-house searches and no hearsay. It wasn't exactly the Brinks Matt gold heist but I felt as if it was – and I'd gotten away with it.

CHAPTER 4

I started a Joke

The Postal Service Con

I'd been at Uni for about 12 months or so up to this point. The classes weren't going very well because I didn't like the subjects I was being taught. Sociology was easy but it just wasn't for me so I didn't apply myself, it was a nothing subject – interesting but for nothing. What was I going to use it for in the real world? The Sports Science and Coaching was the same. None of these jocks were going to go on and be successful in their chosen sport, some of them would go on to be coaches and that would be it.

I had started boxing at the local gym. The first night I went down to check it out; there was a really old guy teaching the boys to box. He was a bit like Mick the trainer from the old Rocky films. The boys were useless but he was pretty cool. He got me to step inside the ring with him and throw some punches while he held his hands up. I didn't want to break the old man so I only threw some light lefts and rights. After a short while he told me that I wasn't punching properly, that there was no power behind the shots and that I was weak. From then on I punched properly.

I trained with the lads for a while, did some sparring and general gym work but it wasn't the same as my Silver Street boxing gym from my home-town. That was a real boxing gym, small and grassroots but real. It stank of stale sweat and hard work and I missed it.

Henry Cooper came to visit once, he said it reminded him of his old days at the beginning of his boxing career. Our 'enry. Almost beat Muhammad Ali by catching him with a left hook – what we called "enry's 'ammer". Fortunately for Ali, after the knock-down Angelo Dundee cut his glove to steal some time so Muhammad could make a recovery. A precious few seconds for him to come back to earth.

You see, in reality, cheats do prosper.

By now my parents had gone through a messy divorce. My mum had taken to partying with her friends pretending she was 21 again and my dad had taken to drink. The family were now split. I felt bad for them but mainly for my siblings. My parents should have split up but not in the way that they did. The environment they'd created for us kids was toxic and my parents were vicious to each other – and to us about each other. They selfishly dragged one another through the mud and took us along for the ride – damaging us all in the process; and with my dad gone, I was free to run wild.

My mum eventually ran off to Spain to re-invent herself for the 87th time. She took my sister with her and split us siblings apart, leaving my brother and me in England. We moved into a shitty flat with my dad on a rough estate. It was the kind of estate where if someone dies then no fucker knows about it until there's a smell. This actually happened with the person in the flat below us.

My dad was in a bad place then and we were always arguing. He drank himself stupid on most nights and would do stupid shit like try and set fire to the flat. I could always escape by lighting up a joint but my little brother had to deal with everything sober.

By now I knew I wasn't biologically related to my dad. This had all come out during the break-up. My cousins had told me some time earlier while on a night out drinking, they had found out from their dad who'd got loose lips from being on the whisky.

I made out I had known the whole time but I didn't have a clue and finding out did something to me inside. From that point on I didn't know where I had come from or who I was supposed to be. I used to look at my clothes and not know how to dress, who the fuck was I? I'd watch sitcoms and analyse the different personalities on screen and would try to determine which of them I most resembled. I didn't know how to be anymore.

Once I had found drugs, I thought I had found myself. Oh, I'm that guy – the stoner that you see in films. I was him. And I got pretty fucking good at it. I ended up in hospital once because I had taken 300mg of morphine and a quarter of an ounce of cocaine. There was still some coke left in the bottom of the bag but I had made a massive dent in it. My body went into shutdown and I remember not being able to move. It started with my fingertips then crept up my arms. I managed to get hold of my dad before it was too late and he came and took me to the hospital. I remember the look on his face when they took me away in a wheelchair – and I hate myself for it. The machine's alarm by my bedside kept going off because my heart rate was off the scale. The coke was trying to take me to outer space but the opiates had other plans.

Speed balling is not for the faint-hearted.

Money was always a problem at Uni. It would be great for the first month or so then everybody would run out of it. The first year you spend in halls, then in the second year you have a house share. My best friend at Uni was Paul, I had met him in fresher's week in a café on campus. He was sat with two guys who were obviously gay – I could tell by the way they had their sideburns cut.

This was something you never saw in my home town. Paul never admitted he was gay the whole time I knew him. He would go out on his own and come back with black eyes and a bullshit flamboyant story saying that some girl's boyfriend had caught him chatting up his girl – when really it happened at some gay bar.

Coming out was still a rare thing then and nowhere near as acceptable as it is now. I never did question Paul about his sexuality – just played along with his harmless bullshit. He was a good guy, intelligent, loud, funny and camp as fuck. He had lots of drive and you could tell that he was going to be someone. He was destined to mix with celebrities in snazzy places, sipping champagne and cocktails in the glitz and glamour.

It was Paul who took me to open my bank account. I didn't like banks or anyone who was dressed smart, for some reason the white collars made me crumble – like they were better than me or something. Paul told me not to be nervous and that he'd help me as soon as I got stuck in conversation – which he did, and we walked out with a Barclays student account with a massive overdraft, my first chequebook, and money to burn. It was time to go on a spending spree.

It didn't take long and it was all gone; it had run dry and money was tight. It had got to the point where a few of us would go through halls, hitting any floors that were unlocked, and steal whatever they had in the fridges and freezers.

The majority of student food was pot noodles, bread, tins and beer. It was Paul who told me that when funds were running low, I could just write a cheque out to myself. When I asked how, seeing as there was no money in my account, he said that there didn't have to be. As long as it was a legitimate cheque and I cashed it in at a post office then it wouldn't matter. So, I did. I wrote myself out a cheque for £50. I took it to the nearest post office and they cashed it. Simple. All of a sudden, I was committing cheque fraud without even knowing what cheque fraud was.

I'm not sure if Paul meant this as a one-time thing – meaning I'd have to replace the funds before the bank caught on – or not. He was a few years older than me and already knew about the banking system. He'd already had various different jobs and was wise to the world, whereas I had only street smarts to rely on. Almost straight away I had ordered myself some fresh new chequebooks – whilst in the calm before the shit storm that would inevitably happen.

As with most other things in my life my nature is to do things at 100 miles per hour. Whether it be taking copious amounts of drugs, alcohol or riding a bike with or without an engine; I have to do it at full speed, take no prisoners and don't look back. I was the kid in the street who built the bicycle ramp as high as it would go, then hit it at full pelt and come crashing down in a pool of blood and broken dreams. I was still juvenile in my scams up to this point, but whatever I had it was on full throttle. Every day I wrote myself a cheque. And every day they cashed it. My confidence would grow each time I did it and it still amazed me every time when they handed me the money, and with a smile. It was brilliant.

I was at my mum's flat when there was a knock at the door. The bank manager of Barclays had himself come looking for me. My mother screamed at me not to let him in – she knew the protocol for the weasels coming to collect. In a very short period, I had amassed over £17,000 in debt from bad cheques alone – not including the thousands I had accrued from a maxed-out overdraft, credit cards and loans. I owed Barclays a small fortune and they were never going to get it. What the fuck were they thinking giving a small-town boy with no understanding of how money worked, who had never really had any to begin with, all this access to thousands of pieces of paper with the queen's head on – it was a recipe for disaster. The bastards had found me. And it was over.

It wasn't long after that I left university. The shit had most definitely hit the fan and I was going downhill very fast. The weed I had been smoking had made me paranoid. At the time I didn't know it was the weed. I thought I was slipping into a combination of genius and madness – of which they say there is a fine line. I would do strange things like sit and organize my VHS video collection, first in alphabetical order, then in genre order – all action videos together, etc. Then start the whole process again. I would sit and write in my journal. At the time I thought it was the work of a genius, like I was coming up with some highly intelligent philosophy that mankind would want to read about, but it was all nonsense. The next day I would go over what I had written and it would be rambling, jumbled up bullshit that didn't make any sense. A bit like the film 23 with Jim Carrey. Obsessive and compulsive, going on and on. I would sit with my guitar and write songs while stoned. At the time I would think they were amazing, that every song would definitely be a number one hit and people would be listening to them and thinking about them as they do Bob Dylan and John Lennon. Then I'd wake up sober, play them and sound more like Yoko Ono – what the fuck was I going on about? I imagine that is what madness is like. The person in it thinks they have all the answers, that they are the next apostle or something and that everyone around them should think and feel the 'truth', the same way THEY do – when really, it's all nonsense, gobbledegook and gibberish.

Campus security found me in my room on my last day. Alongside the weed I had drunk half a bottle of vodka and half a bottle of whisky. I couldn't stop the thoughts in my head so I had decided to call it a day. I cut both wrists with one of the knives I had bought from Spain that was in my drawer. I remember the blade was so blunt that I had to saw through the cuts in the flesh, again and again.

One side was much deeper than the other as on one wrist I had sawn through the tendons, leaving the remaining hand too weak to make a good enough job of it. I do remember closing my eyes thinking this will be it and that would be the end, only to open them the following morning and see campus staff panicking around a bed that was soaked through and stained red. One of my housemates was puking his guts up at whatever he could see and smell. University was well and truly over and done with- along with the weed.

It was now I was diagnosed with anxiety and depression. Looking back, the weed had given me severe OCD, or drastically exacerbated something pre-existing. At first, I thought it was okay, but if I had an issue, or worry, then my mind would obsess over it, going over and over, turning it inside out, to the point where it was exhausted, and way, way over-thought. It's something I still have today, and not managed very well. Since getting 100% sober four months ago, people have told me that I have ADHD. I'm definitely hyper-focused on whatever it is that I'm doing. I will get fixated on whatever the new thing is and spend all my time on it, not wanting to stop and prepare food because it's getting in the way. Then after a period of time it just goes away, dissipates and floats away. Then I'll find something else to put all my energy into.

When I first got sober, I had a lot of time on my hands. I saw a documentary on the Whitechapel murders and Jack the Ripper. The documentary was badly done with terrible research but it was still a good watch and I thought I could do better. In the space of about three months, I must have done the equivalent of about ten years of research for some people. I spent all day and night searching through the internet, collecting crime reports, sketches, eye-witness accounts, newspaper reports and anything else I could find on the subject. I read dozens of books written by other people claiming they knew who the culprit was. Before long I had a small list of suspects, and eventually found who I thought was the murderer who's come to be known as Jack the Ripper.

And that was that. It lifted. I packed up the collection of books I had bought and the folders I had put together because the obsession was gone and the search was over – and more importantly, I could sleep. With university finished, it was time for a brand-new start.

CHAPTER 5

Exist or Not Exist

The Teaching Con

So, I'd come back to my home town licking my wounds and was scratching around for money and a place to stay. On the off-chance I walked into a hotel ran by an Indian family and asked if they had any work going. The owner was a massive guy, bald head with a scar down his face and you could instantly tell he was the man in charge, he called the shots and he wasn't a guy to be fucked with. He sat me down and asked me about my situation. I told him I had nowhere to live, needed work and was willing to start straight away. As luck would have it, they needed a barman. He told me he wanted a white Englishman to run the bar, talk to the customers and serve them drinks.

The rest of the workforce was mainly made up of Polish immigrants who worked for peanuts and sent whatever crumbs they could back home to their families. The big man in charge, Bunny, also employed his nephews to keep the hotel running. They did the admin and reception. They also employed a few young British white girls as waitresses for the same reason they were employing me. Their clientele was aging pensioners who came down by the coach load, they had aged views on different ethnicities so it was better for business that way. I got a live-in job; I could eat whatever food was left over as long as I was on call 24 hours a day and prepared to work 70+ hours per week – with Sundays off to myself. I would get £100 per week in cash and I was to ask no questions and do what I was told.

Looking back, it was definitely slave labour and they had me over a barrel for sure. That being said, the Singh family took me in when I was jobless and homeless, they fed me and gave me a roof over my head. In return I never took advantage of them, never bit the hand that fed me and never took a penny that wasn't earned. I was loyal, hard-working and grateful. The same couldn't be said for the next place.

The hotel I went to after was fucking horrendous. I wished I was still at the previous place working all those hours but Bunny had sacked me on the spot for screwing the waitresses. I didn't argue, I just packed my shit and left. The new place, also ran by an Indian family, was squalid. It looked okay from the front but behind the scenes it was disgusting. The workers here were all immigrants as well, and they all lived out the back in what can only be described as slums. It was dirty, it stank of BO and piss, and it was rat infested. It was like going back to Victorian times to what I imagined London's East End would have been like. I didn't like it from the word go, but needs must. I had a place to stay and no other choice.

I was treated badly from the start and the pay was a joke. It was like water off a duck's back for the rest of the immigrants as they were clearly used to this type of treatment, food and living conditions. I knew I wasn't going to be able to stand it for very long, but in the meantime, I did my yes sir, no sir routine and put my head down on the dirty, sweat-stained pillow which hadn't been washed in, well, forever.

Straight away I was put in charge as head barman working both the top and bottom bars depending on what different functions they had on. I noticed early on that there were cracks in the whole set up. They had CCTV but it was poor, grainy and no-one ever bothered to check them for anything – they were there as more of a deterrent to prevent anyone from getting any ideas about the vast amounts of alcohol in stock. The hotel was busy and understaffed, and it would be hours in-between seeing anyone who thought they were of any importance.

For such a shit hole behind the scenes they were taking money – and lots of it. They held sports functions where minor celebrities turned up to do speeches and sign memorabilia. Henry Cooper came here as well on one of his visits to do a talk and sign some gloves – which were then auctioned off for charity. The jewel in the crown though, was the weddings. Hundreds of drunk people with money to burn and a seemingly endless supply of hard cash. I started creaming off the top almost as soon as I started there – much the same way as I did at the Irish bar before. There was so much money going into the till that I had to keep getting the trays exchanged for fresh ones because the notes wouldn't fit – but I would soon help to alleviate this problem.

I had to figure out a way to get the money away without having to stash it in my pocket because the staff were told to never have cash on them when working because of random searches. All the tips had to be handed in then shared out equally between the staff, the chef and the kitchen staff included – who were behind the scenes and away from the paying customers and their generosity. I came up with the idea of wearing swimming trunks underneath my trousers, they were tight around my legs and nothing would fall out.

You'd be surprised at how much cash you can squeeze into them, undeterred, night after night. At the time I was being paid less than £10 per hour and it was flat out from start to finish. I would try to stick to a 25% take off the top which worked well, went unnoticed for the most part and kept me from walking out like the Michelin man after every shift. I'd worked out where the blind spots from the camera were and became a dab hand at putting money in the till with one hand, and cash down my pants with the other. You think, a wedding catering for three hundred people, if only half of them were paying for drinks at £50 per person over a six-eight-hour period – that's £7,500. And people were paying a lot more than that. Some weddings were there all day and night, with some not finishing until 2am – late licence or not. If people were paying then the bar stayed open.

People get very generous after a few drinks, they buy rounds, and lots of them – with each round costing at least £50 on one order.

It was golden.

I felt sorry for my slum mate Seb. He was working as a waiter and lucky to bring home £80 a night, £75 from his earnings and £5 in tips, and that's for two split-shifts. He knew what I was up to as he'd caught me unloading my Speedos. I supplemented his wages and bought his silence. He wasn't going to tell anyone as it would only mean the payments would stop. It worked for him and it worked for me. Seb and I would often hit the town when our time off hit on the same day. Sometimes it would only be a morning or an afternoon, but we'd go to the pub, play pool, stick the juke box on and spend money like it was going out of fashion.

That was what ended it all for us. We got so smashed one day that we were both unable to make our shifts that evening. I started my shift but was slurring so bad that the customers had complained. Seb didn't even make it down from his room where he'd fallen asleep and puked all over himself. We both got told to leave, they ended up taking Seb back on a week or so later because he wrote a letter of apology. I did as well but the fact that I'd turned up for work pissed was a definite no-no. I should have stayed in bed and slept it off.

We slept in my 3-series BMW I had bought with my extra 'earnings', nice car, red with alloy wheels and twin headlights, boxy E30 shape with comfortable seats – living in a slum and driving a BMW; it made sense at the time.

I few days later I dropped Seb off to be with a girl he had met and I never saw him again.

My mum, now back in England, let me stay for a few nights until I got my shit back together. With the money I had saved from rinsing the hotel I decided it was time for a fresh start, a change of scenery and something away from everything. The only other place I really knew of that was far enough away was Spain, so I packed my bags and headed out for a holiday to start laying some foundations. I stayed with my grandparents for the holiday, they said I could go out and stay for a while, on the condition that I would look for a job and stay off the drugs. I had given up the weed, speed and pills by then so I agreed and started thinking about what I could do to earn a living.

What started off as a long holiday grew week by week. I got a part-time job working in a bar at night paying cash and was painting villas during the day. It was basic stuff, all the villas in Spain were white so it was literally a case of just white-washing them, often with just one coat of paint to brighten them up for ten euros per hour. The bar catered to mainly English but there were Spanish customers as well, so I started to pick up the lingo as I went along – it was only bar lingo really, but it was a start.

The South of Spain in the early to mid-2000s was a good time. It was the chosen destination for ex-crims and ex-pats to get away from whatever shenanigans they were up to in England. My nan had introduced me to a local villain, whose villa she looked after while he was away – on 'business'. He lived up in the mountains in a big posh place with a pool, gated drive with the standard black BMW and Range Rover. Bazza asked me what I wanted to do for work and I told him I didn't know. He asked me if I could drive, which I could, so that was that – I became his driver and would eventually teach his son Maths and English lessons to earn some extra money. Bazza was definitely a good man to have onside, everyone respected him, and everyone was my best friend just because I was associated with him. He would have big dinner parties where all the faces would be invited to – me included – and the fact that I only weighed nine stone at the time, with long hair, didn't seem to matter. My nan thought he sold supplements, they'd had a conversation about what he did for a living and that's what he told her – that he bought them, re-packaged them, and sold them on for profit. He was really into the business of selling cocaine in large quantities and had a lot of guys working for him. Funny really, you wouldn't be in a villa like that and be driven around in cars like that selling re-packaged supplements. My nan was kind of innocent in some ways; that was what he told her and that was what she chose to believe.

Twelve months or so down the line and whatever Bazza had got himself involved in had gone pair-shaped and the shit had hit the fan big-time. In the blink of an eye he and his family were packed up and had to vacate the premises. Everything inside the villa had to be gone, all electricals, designer clothes, food, the lot. In the wardrobe I found a nickel-plated Magnum 357 with black grips. It was a hand cannon and felt twice the weight of the Beretta I'd had back home. It was awesome and would have blown a hole out the arse of anything. I wanted to keep it but it was decided that was probably not the best idea, so one of his partners in crime came to collect. I was, again, without an employer. And with the lifestyle the way it was out in Spain, I needed to get some money, fast.

At this point I still wanted to teach because of my time in the school and the private lessons with Bazza's kid, but I didn't have any real qualifications to do it legitimately so had to put my thinking cap on. I'd been talking to one of the guys in the bar who had a private school in Cartagena, he said he was looking for people to take on for the new school year but would only take on people with qualifications as he ran everything kosher. I found out about an English teaching course but it meant that I would have to fly back to England, stay for a while and complete the course. I didn't have the time it would take to finish the course but like all other things my attitude was fuck it, take a gamble and go and see what happens.

I came back to England and met up with my girlfriend who I was still with and having a long-distance relationship with at this point. She had stayed in England as she was finishing university and planned to come out once her studies were over, which they were coming to and it was almost time. I met up with the guy who ran the teaching course, he was an intelligent and educated man but down to earth and somebody you could properly talk to. I explained my difficulties – that I was living in Spain, had a job potentially waiting for me but not the paperwork, and I didn't have the time to be sitting in a classroom in order to get it. After going back and forth over tea we agreed that he'd give me a tutoring course that was condensed right down into an hour plus the necessary paperwork to take back to Spain – on the condition that we'd never met, that I gave him £500, and that if I ever breathed a word of it to anyone then he'd deny having ever met me.

Now it was back to Spain with my two moody certificates, one for me and one for my girlfriend, who was coming out to meet me. Back in Spain, being that I was applying for a 'proper' job and was on the books, I had to have the right to be working there. Amy and I both applied for our residencia and NIE numbers. I got myself a car, which was only an old Nissan Micra but it was mint, had four wheels and it got me from A to B.

We made our way out to Cartagena to have a look at the school and check out the classrooms. The private school had accepted us both and we were now both officially teachers. Classes were split over the mornings and evenings. It was too hot to work during the day – we didn't have air-con then or at least it wasn't common so everyone went home for a siesta.

I fitted into the role of a teacher quite well, it was the same as I had done in my work experience really, except the kids were Spanish and I was not. There was a bit of a language barrier to begin with but fortunately for us most Spanish kids start learning English early so you're not teaching them from scratch – you're just bettering what they already know. I had to wing a hell of a lot of it as I didn't know myself what a verb, noun, or adjective was, but I was teaching it in the fucking classroom. All I had to do was look right, sound right, and blag right. Which

I did. It was the kids that taught me to speak Spanish. I don't mean the useless shit you read about in the books but the real Spanish; what the locals speak. None of them go into a shop and tell the shopkeeper that they would like to buy some bread and cheese, the same way we don't at home.

The kids taught me their local dialect and how to swear in slang. None of this B-U-E-N-O-S D-I-A-S bullshit. They taught me how to roll Rs and Ls and how to put emphasis on what parts of the word and sentence. I was being paid to learn and they were my best teachers.

Amy never questioned how we had all of a sudden been accepted into a high-paying, quite highly regarded private school where only the posh kids went. She never once asked why it was so easy to get the certificates with little to no experience whatsoever – she either knew and didn't say anything or she was too innocent and it never occurred to her, but I'm guessing the latter. I don't think to this day she knows that we, for quite a considerable amount of time, were working out in Spain on mickey mouse certificates, being responsible for whole classrooms full of kids. Come to think about it, what does a piece of paper prove anyway? Whether you've 'earned' it or not. Some of the most intelligent people I have ever met have never so much as finished secondary school, with some of the thickest fuckers having all the degrees under the sun but don't know how to put a carboard box together. It's all bullshit. Teaching had shown me that if you dressed the part, spoke the part and acted the part – then you were the part.

This got me thinking…

I mentioned earlier about my lifestyle in Spain and my previous employer's business. I guess it was inevitable really that I was going to fall into the path of alcohol, and cocaine. I had stayed away from the weed and not touched it since being out there – I say stayed away; I was growing it in fairly large quantities out the back of my nan's back garden. It started out as a bit of fun between my grandad, the ex-hippie and I, but at 1000 euros a plant, it was hard not to. At the start I was selling it in bars with my grandad coming to deliver it to me in his Renault 4 – then later in bulk quantities to the ex-pats and crims desperate for a smoke. It got to be that I couldn't grow it quick enough to supply the amount of demand that was coming in. And they grew BIG out in Spain, plus you didn't need to pay for any lights or the cost of running them. People were asking for it before it had been chopped and dried. They would even buy it wet, straight off the plant.

By day I was working as a teacher, by night I was a weed salesman and come the weekend I was knee-deep in cocaine.

Everybody who was English frequented a bar. You never saw an Englishman without a beer or an Englishwoman without a glass of wine or a spirit and mixer – everyone was at it. The coke started as a Saturday night thing but it wasn't long before everyone seemed to be on it more days than they were off. Before you knew it, it was every day. I would turn up to class on a Monday morning and be hanging out my arse hungover so it was a sure thing I'd make a grab for whatever the cure was. It became a constant cycle and a regular top up to take away the pain and nightmare. I've always suffered extremely badly when it came to nearly all drug comedowns and hangovers, so when I discovered hair of the dog as a means to a fast recovery it was game over. It wasn't long before I was eight and a half stone, not only skinny but ill-looking and it started to show. I remember one of the kids in the class, a little girl, Belen, called me an 'alcoholico', when I knelt down beside her to help her with her work.

I felt so ashamed – the anxiety got to me in the end and I couldn't turn up for class and take lessons. I didn't have the confidence and found it unbearable; I handed my notice in – I'd blown it.

CHAPTER 6

Didn't Win the Bid

The eBay Multi-Verse Begins

With the loss of my job and the responsibilities that went with it, it wasn't long before I was a complete mess. My girlfriend had caught me in a bar kissing another woman whilst out of my mind. Cocaine and alcohol will do funny things to you. The loose morals that come with too much drink are non-existent when the devil dust is added to the mix. Her sister was out visiting us at the time so within 24 hours her flight was booked and she was gone – six and a half years over just like that.

For the next few months, I drowned my sorrows and snorted as much Columbian marching powder as my wallet could handle, made some poor choices and got balls deep into sex, drugs and rock'n'roll.

What started off as a cheeky gram bought over the bar quickly escalated to visiting the Spanish gypsy camp which was dodgy to say the least. If that wasn't bad enough, it wasn't long before I was making trips out into the middle of nowhere to visit derelict buildings and ordering large quantities through a steel door which only had a gap big enough to pass the money and product through – the kind of place you imagine getting chopped up in and left for dead.

One day my friend Callan and I took mine and my grandparents' cars out into the campo because we were bored. After some cans of confidence and a few lines of disco powder it was decided that the best thing for it was to go banger racing. To be fair, my car had already started to look like it had been in a demolition derby anyway. I'd been out drink driving in it on most evenings and in that time, it had developed a scratch or two; a bit like how Leo DiCaprio's white Lambo looked in The Wolf of Wall Street. I'd reversed it into a no-stop sign outside a bar while out partying with Amy, Callan and Laura.

Another time the car got towed outside the school I was working at; the police thought it had been dumped, but it was still my daily driver and I had to pay to get it back. I remember coming out of the school and thinking where the fuck had it gone, and maybe I'd parked it somewhere else.

The banger racing with mine and my nan's car with Callan was a blast. We'd had a pre-race rule agreement that we wouldn't hit each other's drivers' doors because we didn't have any roll cages inside the cars. This went out the window as soon as we got into it. By the end of it both cars were totalled with one barely running. I used one of them to drag the other back and left them outside my nan's villa. It wasn't long before her phone started to ring with frantic friends concerned that she'd been in a terrible wreck.

My grandparents weren't best pleased. I was told I'd be on the next flight home if I didn't buck my ideas up. As it turned out I would be going back anyway, to get clean and get Amy back. I said goodbye to my friends and said I'd see them soon.

Callan was killed in a hit and run. He was a good friend and one of the best-man trio at my wedding; he was the real deal, loyal, damaged, charismatic, passionate, hardcore and funny as fuck. One time we stripped naked to jump off his mum's roof into the pool, which wasn't deep, and I'm not entirely sure why we had to be naked, other than it was a laugh. Another time I went to visit him in Essex, to save him from himself, I think. I went with the best intentions of picking him up, bringing him back home with me and sorting him out a job. Before I knew it, cocaine had been brought into the mix and we were driving all the way back to Devon to get my passport, to then go on to Prague. I miss that mad bastard.

Three weeks on and I was back home; I'd been meeting up with friends and going out for drinks but the coke was finished with. Amy hadn't wasted any time; she had already met someone else and started a relationship.

It was in a club that I met my future wife, Jean. She approached me and asked if I wanted a drink, I said yes, and that was that. I knew she was older than me so I lied about my age – she knew I was younger so lied about hers. It wasn't until later that we both confessed our sins, but by then it was too late – not that it would have mattered anyway.

I liked Jean the moment I met her. She wasn't trashy or loud, she was quite plain looking but very attractive with wavy, shoulder-length blonde hair. She was dressed in black but not in a goth way or as if she was going to a funeral – kind of Amish, traditional, but with a bit of class. She told me she had a son almost straight away, Ashley, who I'd come to love as my own in time to come.

Within a couple of months, we had moved in together and I had decided I wasn't going back to Spain – Jean was my best friend straight from the start. Before long I was, again, scratching around for money. I joined a job recruitment firm in town and they were finding me odd bits and pieces of work here and there. It was largely dead end, low paid and unskilled work with other no-hopers who didn't have any vision – mostly working in factories and doing jobs that nobody else wanted to do. I would watch these people day after day and you could literally see their souls slowly dying. I had to find something else.

I'd discovered online an auction site where people were listing anything you could think of: clothes, jewellery, antiques – absolutely everything. I'd been to a few auctions before, rubbing shoulders with the tweed crew – but this was different. I could bid for things in my pyjamas in the comfort of my own home, and it was faceless. This was the start of things to come.

Before you knew it, I had built myself up three different eBay accounts, I was listing anything and everything I could get my hands on and I had money coming in. Whatever I made I re-invested on other things and sought bargains in any place that they were hiding.

Ebay was still young then and people were just getting used to it. It was growing faster by the day so I had to get ahead of everyone else before they were all switched on. I noticed cracks in the system – with the site itself and with the users trying to get rich. People were listing at the wrong times so their prized possessions were ending in the middle of the night when most people were asleep. I took advantage of all the mistakes and shortfalls I could and was making money without having to pull any cons. I'd set my alarm so it woke me up at stupid o'clock, so I could be up and bidding at the last second and winning when all else chose to sleep.

I'd list things and hook a few interested parties then bid my own items up so I could max-out whatever anyone wanted to pay – a practice known as 'shilling' or 'shill-bidding'. It worked by artificially inflating the price of an item – thus creating a false impression of higher demand. You only need one person that really wants something and if they have money to burn then you're laughing. Occasionally I would bid it up too high but I could always go back and re-offer it to the people who had the 2nd highest bid and they would always bite, thinking they had nearly missed out on that particular trinket that they oh so needed.

In those days there were no AI hurdles catching anyone out – eBay didn't care anyway, the more you bid something up, the more they made through their percentages. Shilling was brilliant, and there were a good few people at it. It wasn't long before the scam sheisters were flocking in their droves. Things like the 'bait and switch' were appearing. I fell for it at the beginning. You'd order something that looked great then when you got it in the post it certainly wasn't what you ordered onscreen. People were ordering themselves Persian rugs then receiving dolls' house accessories in the post in an envelope – it was quite comical, but it wasn't my style – and not something I would practise. Fake listings, empty box scams, non-delivery items and phishing became commonplace. People were getting messages to pay outside of eBay and buyers were saying things were broken. It soon became a minefield so eBay had to up their game.

For the most part I have always smelled a rat scam before getting stung. There are so many ways a person can give the game away – that's not to say I haven't been caught, which I have – but I never took it personally, well, maybe the once.

A few years ago, I had decided to go 'straight', do something the 'right' way and try earning an 'honest' living for a change. I had got myself a part-time job as a jeweller. I wasn't being paid for my time, my payment would come by way of experience and knowledge in the jewellery game, with a few empty promises thrown in for good measure. I already had a good level of self-taught education in precious metals and gemstones. I knew all about the 4-Cs when it came to diamonds; the 'cut' – being a diamond shape, round, oval, princess, etc; the 'colour' – ranging from D-Z, white/colourless, to yellow, then brown, which would be palmed off as 'fancy', or 'cognac' diamonds; the 'carat' – meaning a diamond's weight, 0.01, 0.1, 1, 2, 3 carats in size; and 'clarity' – talking about how pure a diamond is and how free it is from inclusions, whether it is internally flawless or fully fucked. I already knew about a diamond's make-up, its origins and what each part of it was named, its facets, table, crown, girdle, pavilion, culet and whether it was old, European or rose-cut.

For such a small stone there is a lot to learn and that is just the tip of the iceberg. I already knew about precious metals, gold, rose gold, white gold, platinum, silver, their hallmarks and what they meant, the precious metal content, year of manufacture and so on.

Andy was the boss; he was to become my supposed partner in time, teach me anything I didn't already know and polish up my skills.

One of the perks of my job would be that any work I needed doing on any piece of jewellery – a repair, a re-size, a stone replacement, cleaning or stone setting would be done for free – something I would soon be taking advantage of.

I decided I was going to get my own diamond rings made up and sell them, either from the shop, or online. I had already spotted in the shop display windows, being the obsessive magpie that I was, that there was a huge mark up on what jewellery was being sold for, compared to the actual cost that any particular piece was to make.

Through my experience in the shop, I knew how much it cost to have jewellery repairs done; which was pennies compared to what we were charging the customer. I know that there is a cost involved which is to pay for overheads. The customer is not only paying for that piece of jewellery, they are also paying for the shop lease, the electric bill, fuel, post, phone bill, internet, paper, pens and anything else that it costs to keep the shop running. That being said, what was costing us £5-£10 for a very minor repair, we were charging £50-£100, and with stone replacement we could charge almost what we liked. I know this is the same in any skilled profession but this was through the roof.

I'd look in other High Street jewellers and see they were selling engagement rings for £5,000, £10,000, £15,000, £25,000. And the stones in them were terrible, they were grey and hazy, with some almost black – like they had just been brought up from the coal mine. And people were buying these?!

It's pretty shocking how ill-informed the general public are when it comes to precious gems and how much people are willing to spend their money on, which is essentially shit that has come from the ground – a piece of coal that has formed over time with some heat and pressure, then polished and cut and put into a thin piece of shiny metal to prove to someone how much you love them – absolute nonsense. However, if people wanted to spend their money, then I planned to help relieve them of some of it. The British public were going to get the bargain of a lifetime – all honest and above board.

I'd been given a copy of the shop manual to use as a reference with the customers when picking out a ring design, because at the shop, not only did we do repairs but we also could make a ring to your specifications and you could pick out the style of mount you wanted. I'd ask about how much we were buying these mounts in for, which turned out to be in the region of between £150-£250 – slap a stone in it with a useless piece of paperwork and bob's your uncle, 'that'll be £10,000 please, sir, would you be paying by cash or credit card?'

I'd also ask about where the diamonds would be coming from but was met with unclear answers, he wasn't going to be giving away all his secrets just yet. I'd already seen on my newfound auction site that they were selling diamonds on there, most with their very own useless pieces of paperwork to 'guarantee' their importance and 'authenticity'.

Online you could get a one carat round brilliant cut stone, D-G colour, which was okay & SI clarity (slightly included), which was fine to the naked eye, for anywhere between £300-£600, Throw in a mount, £150-£250, some paperwork (pennies), a box (a few pounds), and the cost of a stone setting (£10). So, for £450-£850 you were getting a better end product compared to half the shit in the window displays costing anywhere between £5,000-£25,000.

Easy money.

So that was what I did. I ordered some diamonds, and they came through, and they were great. On some of them the colour was a shade different to what they said in the description, but they were fine. I chose mainly round brilliant cut stones because they were the most popular, and I ordered some mounts that were simple and classic looking. I had the diamonds set into the mounts, which were all size 'N', as that was the most common size (which could be re-sized later anyway). I ordered some nice black ring boxes and got each one appraised, 'for insurance purposes only' – written in the small print. This basically gives you permission to jack up the price of any piece of jewellery and gives the buyer a false sense of worth and value of said stone and chunk of metal – something the guys loved to see and the girls always fell for.

The finished product was awesome – they were far better than what I had seen in some of the High Street shops and I'd got them done for a fraction of the price. I thought if I could sell them for £2,000 a piece then I'd be making more than 100% profit and the buyers would be over the moon with their savings – but could I sell them? Could I fuck. I listed some online, a few sold but the majority didn't, which I didn't understand. I had built up a lot of sales, with a lot being jewellery and I'd had 100% positive feedback. I put some of them in our shop window which is where they stayed. People in my home town started to get nervous if they were paying anything over £20, let alone £2,000. I had potentially £50,000 worth of stock that I was selling at rock-bottom prices, but my money was tied up and they weren't selling. It turns out that even if you do have actual gold and diamonds, if you're in the wrong place then you're wasting your time. If I'd had a shop in Hatton Garden then they would have flown off the shelf and I would have been laughing all the way to the bank, but it wasn't to be – not yet anyway.

I'd had my fair share of scammers as well. I saw most of them a mile off – the usual requests to deal outside of eBay, the PayPal scams – where they'd offer more than what you were asking, then put that amount into your PayPal account. The trouble was, the amount was a request and not a paying amount – that way you end up paying THEM the £2,000, AND losing a diamond ring.

There was one particular guy that tried it on; he was foreign. I'd had my doubts because of this, with his bad use of English – which isn't fair and discriminatory, but going by previous dealings it didn't fill me with confidence. Anyway, this guy had paid the full asking price, which was £2,000, I had my concerns so contacted eBay and asked them what they thought. An eBay rep contacted me and went through the security checks and they told me he was legit, had been dealing on eBay for a long time, had excellent feedback history, etc, etc, and to go ahead with the sale. Just to be sure I asked him to send me two forms of identification with his name, photo and address on – which he did, begrudgingly. I sent the engagement ring, box and evaluation appraisal and all seemed good, the eBay rep had been right – until a few weeks later. Then I received the message, 'Why you sell me fake diamond, I want money back, you scam me'. Instantly I was enraged. The diamond was legit, the mount was fully hallmarked gold, the box was good and the paperwork was as honest as any other jeweller's appraisal, and this fucker was trying to rip me off.

I found the address of his home and place of work (which were on his ID cards I had requested), I also found the name and address of the nearest jeweller to him and I got photos of them all. All that was needed was to simply send a message and attach all three photos, and to say to take the ring to that jeweller around the corner from him to get the ring looked over. He understood the threat – silent as it was but he knew I was onto him, knew where he lived and that I'd be on my way. I knew he would cower – which he did. And with that he apologised, said it had been his mistake and then thanked me afterwards. He was a scoundrel, a sheister, a wannabe scamster of the lowest kind – and it wasn't going to be tolerated. You don't scam an individual for vast amounts of money; there are rules and it isn't right. For all my efforts I hadn't made much money and there was no end of uphill's, pitfalls and headaches. That was the end of going legit and above board.

It wasn't worth it.

CHAPTER 7

He Likes the Tom Foolery

The Gold Sovereign Con

I've been interested in gold for as long as I can remember. There is something about it which has allured us to its beauty for thousands of years. I still like it – but I don't know why. Is it because, like you, I have been hypnotized into thinking it is something I want, and need? Is it because I have been manipulated into thinking it is a precious, rare commodity? It can be pretty, but let's face it, if you melt copper and zinc and combine them together then you are going to come up with something that looks, feels and weighs pretty much the same. Then again copper and zinc do not have much of a history, do they? That, and there's plenty of it. Why is white gold more valuable than silver? They look almost the same. Why is platinum more expensive than white gold? They look the same. And why is platinum way more expensive than silver? They look the fucking same! Rarity. What is going to happen when electric cars become commonplace? They're going to be needing a hell of a lot of silver – start investing in silver NOW, while it is plentiful and cheap. You heard it here.

Mark my words.

I've also been interested in gold coins for years. Back in the old days we used gold coins in everyday money, for some classes anyway. The sovereign and guinea for the UK, the gold eagle in the US and the Krugerrand in South Africa – and for years we've been right little scamsters. Back in the day people used to file off the edges, which is why coins have a milled/ridged/reeded edge to this day. For precious coins it is to try and stop 'clipping' – filing off some gold dust and collecting it for later. For other, less precious coins it is to stop counterfeiting. Although, it hasn't stopped people from trying.

Most of the gold guineas you see now have all been clipped in the past. If you came across a bunch of guineas and shaved a small amount from every single coin it would soon mount up. To buy one full guinea in this day and age that hasn't been clipped – at all – is unheard of and would cost you an arm and a leg for one coin, and that is because everybody was at it. For years we've been pilfering, conning, scamming and scheming, and we will continue to do so for many years to come. My antics will soon be outdated and the digital age will be here to stay – and so will the scammers.

I bought my first gold sovereign with my university study money. It was a lot smaller than I thought it would be, and it didn't weigh much – just under eight grams of 22 carat gold. I can't even remember how much it cost me, but it was nowhere near as much as it costs for one in this day and age. I instantly wanted more, and I instantly wondered if there was a way of acquiring some – or at least what looked like some.

It wouldn't be until a few years later I would get the chance, at my first auction. I had gone there to take a brooch that my nan had given me from her collection of costume jewellery. I had picked it out and told her that I thought it was valuable; she disagreed but said I could have it. I took it to a jeweller in town to get a second opinion. He asked if it was for sale; I said no. He then told me it was French, antique, and was worth £400-£450. I let my nan know – she was happy, and still said for me to keep it and sell it on, so I put it into auction.

To cut a long story short, the brooch sold for £30 and I was gutted – I hadn't put a reserve on it and had faith that others would know of its value – but they didn't, and a very large woman with a peculiar hat had a very good day indeed. After fees I was in it for even less, which was not a good day at the office – but all was not lost.

Two good things came out of the auction that day. One was to learn a very valuable lesson with auction listings; the other was the collection of replica gold-plated sovereign coins I took home with me. So, with my tail between my legs I went home thinking about how I was going to get my money back.

I got home and looked at the coins. Seeing as nobody else was interested, they looked good, were the right diameter and thickness, the milled edges were crisp and they had come from a good cast. The problem with them was the weight. They weighed seven grams, which was 0.98 of a gram too shy and they would be found out in an instant. I set about looking for mounts to put them in.

After quite a bit of searching I found a guy in America who was selling necklace coin mounts mainly for Krugerrands of all different sizes and he was willing to sell for a very low price if I was to buy in bulk. At the time there was rarely custom fees to pay, so I ordered a bulk load, they arrived and more importantly, with a bit of jiggery pokery, they fit. I found another dealer who was selling gold chains, all hallmarked, who was also willing to sell for rock-bottom prices if I bought only 16" chains and in large quantities. At the time it worked out I'd be buying each chain for less than £10 so with the mounts I was in for about £30 a pop.

I took them all to my jeweller friend and he soldered each mount up so they were locked shut, but looked great. I hunted around for ring mounts as well. There were some about but they were much more expensive. I bought what I could, took them along to my friend as well and had the same done to them. Before long I had what looked like a Pirate's treasure chest full of booty ready for the off. Now all I had to do was sell them, and by the looks of it, it would take a lifetime. However, within a week, they were gone.

With regards to my cons to come this was small potatoes and still within the nickel and dime era and something I did for fun. That being said, it was still profitable, netted me a number followed by zeros and beat working in a factory. I listed them online, through word of mouth and on social media. I'd also been brazen enough to take a few to my local auction house – the same place I had bought them from in the first place sometime prior. They sold like hot cakes, people were buying them for their girlfriends, themselves and their bits on the side. Nobody complained (except the auction house) and I never lied. Online I listed them as 'solid gold chain with gold sovereign coin mount and coin' with no mention of the words 'sovereign coin', just sovereign coin MOUNT with coin. People for the most part didn't notice or seem to care. Their mothers and other halves were happy, their wallets were happy and I was happy.

As a bit of a social experiment, I would get talking to the people I sold to in person. I'd ask them if sovereigns were worth much money – and they all said the same: 'No'. It was just something their partner liked, or it was 'just' something they'd had before, for nostalgia, or to replace the coin they'd lost from another pendant. By them thinking they were having one over on me, they were doing the job for me.

It turns out it is very easy to fool the fool who thinks he is fooling you. And knowing that they thought they were ripping me off, made it all that much easier to take their money. Money for old rope- money for gold-plated brass. I pulled the sovereign scam a few more times and incorporated other gold coins into the mix like the Krugerrand but they didn't seem to go as well as the British coins. Before long, it had started to lose traction and by then I had gotten bored of it and wanted to move on to the next endeavour.

For some reason I have always been the same. I'll get something in my head and put all my energy into it. To the point where it consumes me. It's all I can think about and I will spend every waking hour fixated on whatever it is. Then after a while, it will dissipate and the obsession will fade away. At that point I am no longer interested, and I move onto something else. What is that?

When I was a kid, I was constantly changing my mind about who and what I wanted to be when I grew up. I'd watch Days of Thunder with Tom Cruise and want to be a race car driver, then Commando with Arnold Schwarzenegger and I'd want to be in the army, then Top Gun, a pilot, Rocky, a boxer, and so on. I would obsess about being whatever they were onscreen, and that too, would be 100mph for however long it lasted and eventually it would fizzle out and go away, until the next thing cropped up. I have always done it since a child, and I continue to do it as an adult. It's both the bane of my life and my superpower at the same time.

When I was growing up, I looked to my dad but felt a long way away from him. I would watch him and my brother working on cars together in the back garden and I longed for that connection that they had. The fact of the matter is I wasn't interested in engines. I wanted to go and play with my friends and ride my bike, build jumps and hit them as fast as I could. I didn't want to be under the bonnet of a car. But I wanted to want to, if that makes sense.

Growing up, my brother and I were very close. Although born five years apart, we were inseparable as kids and did almost everything together. I always felt, and still do, very protective of him. When we were at the house in Ritcroft we would have a babysitter while my mum and dad went out for the night. She was only 15 and the daughter of our next-door neighbour. After they'd gone, she would start with the weird shit. She would tell me to kiss her which I didn't want to because I was shy. She wouldn't force me to do it like the other sick fucks on the estate but she would do something different. She would try and use my brother as a manipulation tool. If I didn't kiss her, she would tell my brother to kiss her instead, and so on. It was a long time ago but I can still remember the way my brother kissed her. The way a toddler does it because they haven't learned to pout properly yet. They kind of put their lips together then go in for a kiss with their mouth wide open. I remember then feeling protective, that I wanted her to leave him alone. I knew it wasn't right but I didn't know why because she did it in a 'kind' way – with a smile. She would start with the kiss and try to move onto other things – basically showing and touching.

That time I was strong enough to say no – and she didn't push it. I don't know exactly where the line between inappropriate and abuse is, but I think she was pretty much on it. My brother was barely out of nappies and hadn't been walking long. Thank God no harm ever came to him. He was too good to be damaged, and he isn't – despite carrying some scars. Watching him succeed and bring up his own family has been a blessing.

CHAPTER 8

World Chump

The Boxing Memorabilia Con

This con came about through my love of boxing and my means of sales through the eBay stratosphere. It was simple, easy, and pretty much anyone could have done it – which they did, do, and will continue to do in future. But I did mine on a bigger scale.

It started with a genuine purchase. I was on the lookout for some boxing memorabilia to go alongside my trophies and photos from my boxing days that I had found in a box from when we'd moved house. I'd thrown some of it out and dismantled one of the trophies, so the boxing figures could be used to put on a birthday cake for my old underworld boss on his birthday; it was a boxing ring with the two fighters and my cut-up trophy did the job.

I liked the old-school fighters from back in the day and one of my favourites was Jake LaMotta aka The Bronx Bull. He wasn't a particularly flashy fighter and wasn't known for his finesse, but what he lacked in skill he made up for in hard work and courage. He was the first fighter to beat Sugar Ray Robinson – widely regarded as the best pound-for-pound fighter that has ever lived. Sugar

Ray and LaMotta had a huge historic boxing rivalry and fought six times between 1942 and 1951. Robinson won these series of fights by 5-1 but all were very close and every one of them was a war. Robinson's loss to LaMotta would be his first and only loss and remain that way for nearly a decade.

I had seen online whilst scrolling through that a signed Jake LaMotta robe had come up for sale. It was leopard print and it came in a frame with a certificate of authenticity. I purchased it immediately and waited for it to arrive from America. In the description it said that Jake had signed it at a particular event that he had visited, which I checked out; and he had in fact been to the event to do some signing. There was even a photo of Jake signing the robes that were made from the same style leopard print. It looked good.

When the robe arrived, it was made from new, cheap material, it came in a cheap frame with Perspex and the signature was written in marker pen. Along with it came the C.O.A., freshly printed from someone's computer and very poorly done, with another signature that I couldn't make out. The certificate and the robe both had a matching hologram sticker on them, to prove that they were the genuine article. I knew the instant I opened it that it was fake – but I put it up on the wall anyway, because I wanted to believe it was the real deal. People would come round and ask about it and I would tell them. It was a great conversation piece but I knew, deep down, it was bullshit. It didn't make me mad though; it gave me an idea. I went back to the seller and read through their feedback and to my amazement people were falling for this shit, they were charging astronomical prices and everyone seemed happy. I had made far more convincing certificates myself and given them away for free. They sold sheets of holograms on the same site I was looking on, along with the frames and anything else I needed.

The boxing memorabilia con was born – and mine was going to be bigger, much, much bigger.

With some research on what was selling and how much they were selling for, I decided on the fighters I wanted to use. Muhammad Ali merchandise was selling for thousands but I didn't want to go down that road for two reasons: firstly, the name was too big, people would be scrutinizing the credentials a lot more; and secondly, I wasn't comfortable screwing individuals for thousands of pounds.

There were other names about that would sell for a few hundred and there would be no questions asked for the majority of sales. Like my dad always said: 'look after the pennies and the pounds will look after themselves', well that's what I planned to do, except to look after the hundreds so the thousands could be looking after each other.

I set about looking for things to be 'signed'. I started buying up old boxing gloves, the old leather kind, usually brown – that smelled the same as my old club, stale sweat. You could get these for next to nothing at all because they were relics, and not many people would be wanting to train with them. With a pair of old gloves, it was like two for the price of one as I would be getting two sales from each pair. I ordered a shed load of display boxes, decent ones, some wood and some glass, others plastic and Perspex. But nothing thin, cheap looking or rubbish. I printed off C.O.A.s by the bucket load and had them stacked up ready to go. I ordered as many pairs of shorts as I could get hold of, starting with old, classic ones from the 50s, 60s, 70s and 80s, until they had run dry so I was forced to buy newer. I sat and practised each of the boxer's signatures and got Jake's down to a fine art. It was clear, swirly and easy to do once you got it right. And there couldn't be any mistakes because it was thick, black marker pen and it wouldn't come off once applied.

Like with the LaMotta robe that I had researched, I found where the boxers had been to signings and got the dates of where and when each signing had taken place. The product was good, much better than some of the other shit that was out there, and it sold – fuck me it sold. What started off as bedroom signing soon became a full-time job. I had gloves, vests, boots, robes, display boxes, certificates and frames stacked up to the ceiling. The postmen were constantly at my door, and I was forever going to the post office to send away the goods. It got to the point where I actually did give up my day job and got some extra help in. No way was I going to be working for £10 an hour slogging my guts out when I had a licence to print money from home. I had to be a bit careful online, it would've looked too suspicious having one seller immediately flooding the market with goods so I employed three other people who each had their own eBay accounts. All they had to do was write a brief description of what they were selling, then send each item in the post, the same way I did. For their troubles each got 20% of the final sale price so it was in their interest to make the descriptions good. The more they made, the more I made and everyone's a winner. Even the guy who ends up with it last. He has a good product which he has bought for a good price and he has a great conversation piece that looks more real than if it had been kept by the corner man himself.

There are no doubt hundreds and hundreds of signed pieces still hanging in people's bedrooms, man-caves, fireplaces and gyms. Thanks to Willie Pep, Jake LaMotta, Harry Greb, Ted 'kid' Lewis, Henry Cooper and many more – you have made lots of people happy with your name on their precious items and keep sakes. Whether or not you intended to, and with a little help from me, we brought memorabilia to the masses and at an affordable price. Considering it is just ink on leather or fabric at the end of the day, the same as the ink on my certificates – it is only real if you think it is.

Eventually the people I had working for me got greedy, they took from the top – which I knew they would, eventually. Everybody does. They took too much, and in the end, greed gets to everyone. You're happy with what you have for a little while and then the novelty wears off – 20% at the beginning seems like a good deal, but before long you want 30%, then 40%. It's addictive, the same way a drug is. At first a little is enough to get you high, but then you have to take more of it to get the same effect – until the point where you need a shit load and you don't feel a thing. It's exactly the same, and what goes up, will eventually, inevitably come crashing down at some point. It always does.

I'd stayed clean of drugs for the most part since meeting Jean, but there were a few odd occasions where the white powder would make an appearance at a party or special occasion. Synthetic cocaine had made its way onto the scene by this point as well, so what was costing £50 a gram before was costing you £10 a gram now. And it was evil, cheap, man-made, trippy nastiness that was way worse. It fucked a lot of people up in my home town and gave them all manner of mental health problems which affected everyone.

I had no problem staying illicit drug free but as soon as I started it was very hard to stop. One night became a three day+ bender very easily and I always found it hard to get off the train once on it. Why have two drinks when you can have 15? Why one gram when you can polish off an 8-ball? It never ends, until there is carnage and you're too worn out to carry on. My limit would be six weeks. Six weeks of straight 100mph partying until the zombie apocalypse. Six weeks of hardly any sleep and barely any food and you're done. Shrivelled up and looking old and worn, mentally ill with bones that are sore and with ribs showing. The party eventually has to end, and you come down with a crash – realising the shit you have caused in the wake of devastation from your actions. Now all you have is empty apologies, depression and sorrow. But it seemed fun while it lasted, at least at the start.

The boy was growing as well. I had to be as normal as possible because he was around. I still drank, a little too much, but then most of my family did, especially at the weekends. I had to stop growing weed because he had started to ask questions. I was growing it in the bedrooms but it didn't take long for him to start asking about the wardrobes and why we had so many of them. I moved the operation into the garages but he started to ask about the lights and the electricity so I had to call it a day. A shame really, such easy money at £1000 a plant for very little work. I'd proven time and time again that money could be grown on trees if there aren't any other obstacles in the way. We still laugh today about the 'tomatoes' I used to grow back in the day. Maybe I should have thought back then about the future conversations I'd be having, a bit like how my parents should have thought back in their day about how some things would come back to bite them in the arse eventually. Never mind, no harm done, not with the plants anyway.

It was time to be thinking about another venture. So far, I had produced, spent and sold counterfeit money, conned my way into owning my first Rolex, de-frauded Barclays out of hundreds of bad cheques, scammed my way into teaching at a private school, flooded my home town in fake gold bullion, and become the heavyweight champ in the field of iffy boxing memorabilia – but it wasn't enough. I needed my next score, the next hit – and it had to beat the last, and it was staring me in the face the whole time.

For years now I had been playing the guitar. My grandad had given me his, he'd bought it with his first week's wages. It was a harmony, and he had made it into an electro-acoustic with one pick up. My grandad used to play in a skiffle group and grew up listening to Lonnie Donegan and skiffle music, alongside rock'n'roll. That's where my love for rock'n'roll grew, as I already listened to it as a kid because of what my dad and my uncle played in their old cars. My grandad taught me to play three chords, A, D and E, and said that with them I'd be able to play a whole array of rock'n'roll and most of what Buddy Holly had written and performed.

The harmony was a great guitar to start learning with, because it was one of the hardest guitars to play – but I didn't know it at the time. The action was really high and the strings cut your fingers like cheese wire – something most guitars will do at the start because you haven't built up the callouses yet in your fingertips. But not like this though – this was razor wire and you needed what seemed like 50 pounds of force to push the strings down close enough to the fretboard in order to get a good sound out of it – but once you had mastered it, you could play any guitar under the sun, effortlessly.

I played around with the guitar over the years and briefly had another of the many pipe dreams of becoming a singer/songwriter. I wrote an album which mainly consisted of what my father would call suicide music – but I wrote what was in my head and that was unfortunately all that would come out. The songs were good, I liked the chord progression, choruses, build up and flow but my dad was right – it was suicide music.

I bought various tape recorders over the years; my favourite was the Tascam 4-track tape deck with frequency dials which took cassette tapes and had ports that you could connect up your mic and amp with a jack plug. You really felt like you were going to be on Top of the Pops once you got one of those bad boys fired up. They eventually fizzled out and CD recorders came in. It was never going to go anywhere anyway. I never had the confidence to sing in front of anyone which kind of fucks it from the start really. The only time I was ever confident enough was when I was wasted and couldn't string a sentence together.

As the years rolled on and money started coming in, I was able to progress from my first acoustic with attitude to something better, at first starting with a Yamaha which was followed by a succession of guitars right up until I got the holy grail, a Martin D-28. If it was good enough for Johnny Cash, John Lennon and Elvis Presley, then it was definitely going to be good enough for me. It was 20 years ago and it cost me £2,000 then – it wasn't new but it looked it, had barely been played and had spent years in a display cabinet. The fucking thing could play itself; it was that good. It had that dreadnought 'boom' that only a dreadnought guitar has with its distinctive shape. This got me thinking – it's only wood, metal strings and tuners, right? I'd just paid £2,000 for mine, happily paid for it as well. In fact, I couldn't have given my money away quick enough for this mass-produced piece of musical equipment that essentially didn't look all that different to the Ibanez stood next to it. And that sounded awesome as well. Similar looking wood finish, same style, different names.

Hmm, I wonder...

CHAPTER 9

The Little Bird with The Big Heart

The Gibson Con

I was 19 when it happened. Amy and I had moved into a flat to start our third year at university which I was never going to complete but didn't know it at the time. As far as I was concerned, I'd wing it for the final year and come out with a shit degree, but it would be okay because I would still be able to prove I had applied myself to something and completed it. I took a shower the same as I did every morning but this morning in particular would change my life. I had been smoking heavily the night before, which was nothing new, but for some reason or other the powers that be had decided my Cheech & Chong days were about to take a turn on me.

It happened in an instant. I looked down at my feet and they looked strange for some reason, like they didn't belong to me. I lifted my feet up and put them down again, then splashed them down into the water and shook my head whilst closing my eyes and then looked at them again. They were still weird, like I was low key tripping. My toes looked strange, like they were little people lined up together, ten little faces all stood up in a line. Then I looked down at my hands, at my fingers, and they were the same. I didn't know it at the time but this was to be my first day of dealing with depersonalisation/derealization – it would go on to become a lifelong battle with post-traumatic stress, with thousands of episodes of panic attacks to keep good company. A long, drawn out nightmare that I would deal with in the only way I knew how – more drugs.

It would take a further two years to finally give up the weed. At the time I didn't know it was the cannabis. I thought I was just stressed out. None of my mates suffered with any of this at the time, or so I thought, and after all, weed calms you down, doesn't it? It took the very near successful suicide attempt for me to finally call it a day.

Alcohol would find its way in though and would help for a little while – well, it was great while I was under the effects of the alcohol. But I couldn't be pissed all day every day, unfortunately – society tends to thrown upon those people, but it wouldn't stop me from trying though. I spent from the age of 21 to 39 intoxicated, every, single, day. Apart from the times that I spent in hospital or at home on various alcohol detox programmes.

My first ever detox was in my late 20s. I had never wanted to be a piss-head, I hated it, hated alcohol, hated others with a drink problem, absolutely everything about it – but it was a remedy. Both the cause and the cure to many of life's problems. It was time to address the problem as I had given myself alcoholic neuropathy – basically nerve damage caused by chronic alcohol consumption and malnutrition. I went to drive the car one day and when I pushed the clutch down on the car my foot wouldn't do what my brain was telling it to do. At first, I just thought I had a dead leg so didn't think much of it; unfortunately, the leg stayed dead for months and I had to walk with crutches because of the foot drop. Thankfully some feeling came back; it's never fully come back to life but it scared me into getting some help.

A nurse came to my house the first time to start my ten-day course that I'd been on a waiting list for months for. It started well but a day in and my uncle died in a motorcycle accident. I was very close to him; he was the president of a motorcycle club and closely affiliated with the Hells Angels. His funeral was a week later. As far as funerals go it was awesome. My dad rode a trike which my uncle had built for him. He led the pack of bikers which made up the funeral procession. Bikers came from miles around to show their respects. Some of the Hells Angels rode up ahead and stopped the traffic at each roundabout so all the bikers could get through. It was cool as fuck. I couldn't be around this lot as well as family and deal with what had happened.

I had to drink.

My second detox was in my early 30s. I had managed to curb my drinking and had started to spar and train with my brother again. We went up to the boxing club and joined for one last comeback. As always, I was put back straight back into the ring, not ready, and definitely not match fit. My soft tissue was torn in my ribs in the second round and it was instantly game over. I carried on for another two rounds but my body was shot and it would take months to heal.

It was an old surfing injury that had resurfaced, the waves kept pulling me back into the sea as I was trying to stumble out. Every time I got myself up out of the water the waves would come in and drag me over the pebbles and pull me back each time. It was high tide and the waves were 10-12 ft. Far too big for my skill level. I shouldn't have even been in the water that night and it was the closest I have ever come to drowning.

The second detox went like a dream – it was brilliant. This time it was in hospital and I had a team of doctors and nurses assisting me through it. Like the home visits I was given a massive dose of chlordiazepoxide and gradually weaned off over the ten days. I was eight stone five pounds and very poorly when I first arrived at the hospital, but I came out looking like a different person. It lasted a month until I was back drinking again – a waste of resources and efforts from the medical team but I still wasn't ready.

The third detox was again at hospital in my late-30s. By now my liver had blown up like a balloon. It was nothing like the first hospital visit. It was a chaotic nightmare that happened around Covid, the medical staff were stretched and nobody seemed to know what they were doing. My chlordiazepoxide doses were given out randomly and in no particular order so I had to work the staff, get as many doses as I could, then hide the capsules and work out my own schedule. I did it and came out two days shy of the course end date because they needed the beds.

It was horrific, I had contracted Covid in hospital, my Covid fever alongside my detoxing had made my heart rate go tachycardic and kept setting the alarms off. My body temperature was in the low 40s and I was not in a very good way. Again, I came out looking much better than I went in, but again, it didn't last. This time my abstinence lasted around six months until I was back drinking.

My fourth and fifth detox I did at home, cold turkey. These two detoxes have caused me long term internal damage but I wouldn't remove them from my life because it was those horrifying experiences that have made me not go back. The last one burnt all my oesophagus from constantly being sick, with the stomach bile burning as it came out. I wouldn't wish these experiences on my worst enemy. They have definitely taken years off my life, but the hell was necessary, and I know I am not healthy enough to go through it again.

I think in the end you hit rock bottom and one day you decide you've finally had enough of all the suffering. I will never, ever, go through that again.

My very first detox is what introduced me to benzodiazepines. Valium is like alcohol in a tablet and it is great because you cannot smell it, if you dissolve it under your tongue it works in minutes, you don't get hungover, it gives you confidence, doesn't ruin your stomach, and doesn't get you snogging fat women in bars – but it is the devil in disguise. I was addicted to Valium for ten years and at my worst I was taking just over 100mg daily, which is enough to fuck up a horse.

Giving up alcohol was a walk in the park compared to giving this shit up. It would take me around two years to ween off of it in very small doses at a time. The rule of 10-4-6. You need to give up 10% of your daily dose every four to six weeks. It doesn't matter if it's diazepam, clonazepam, lorazepam or Kazakhstan – 10% every four to six weeks. And with each drop you won't even know you've dropped for a good few days because of the long half-life of the tablets (for diazepam). This would then be followed by two weeks of depersonalisation/ derealization, then a week or so of feeling okay, just in time for the next drop in dosage.

Oh yes – depersonalisation. Ten years addicted to Valium, almost 19 years addicted to alcohol and five years addicted to weed. They're all fucking horrible, they have caused me no end of mental trauma which I hope I will one day beat. I thought they helped me at the time – which they did. But it took me far too long to understand that what was going up would come crashing back down, and when it did it would take everything in its path. Thank fuck that shit is over with. Now all I have to do is pick up the pieces after my very own hurricane Katrina and will my way back to eternal enlightenment.

So, depersonalisation/ derealization. My first episode of dp/dr (low key tripping) happened at 19 in the shower; my first serious attack (full on, balls deep, who the fuck am I and why do I feel like I've nailed a thousand magic mushrooms) happened when I was 21. They would carry on happening throughout my 20s and 30s which is why I carried on drinking – I was petrified of them.

I have learned to cope with them but I still have flare-ups – depending on what stressors are happening in my life at any particular time. I had one today, because I had to sit in a car with two people that I'm not particularly comfortable with. It can happen in a crowded room, if I'm put in charge, in a lift, on an escalator, on my way to a meeting – basically any situation that I feel trapped in and can't make a getaway. But I will beat it, it's just the mind's defence mechanism for when it's stressed out and doesn't want to deal with what's going on.

I am sober, I haven't drunk for two and a half years and I haven't used Valium in months. There is a light at the end of the tunnel and I am stronger than I think. I just need to believe in myself; the same way others do. I'm telling you this for reasons that will make sense when we delve a little further. Which brings me to my next scam, and this time it involves guitars.

By now I hadn't pulled a scam in a while. I was getting my life back together and started working a job as a heavy machine driver at a wood and metal sorting centre. The pay was shit but a monkey could do the job, plus it would get me out of the house and talking to people again. As with many underpaid, undervalued and overworked jobs it can be worth it if you have a brain that can think outside the box. There are lots of goods passing hands at this facility and what looks very much like junk can be another man's treasure if it is put into the right hands.

We took tonnes and tonnes of metal every day, ferrous and non-ferrous. It's surprising how much copper would be coming in, in vans loaded up to the rafters by people who probably complained that they were skint – whilst throwing away money that was literally right in front of them.

They would throw antique furniture into the wood container, some of it still in good nick and easily re-sellable just as is. Some people really cannot see the wood for the trees. And the silver and gold, people would actually bring in jewellery and throw it away. Gold, you're throwing away fucking gold?! Some people deserve to stay poor, and it's not surprising why they are. Let's just say the job had it perks.

As I looked down at my beautiful Martin D-28 that I had spent more money on than some people would have a car, I was struck by how similar it looked to the Ibanez that was stood next to it. How the fuck can one cost under £100 and the other thousands? It's wood and strings for fuck's sake. I had a look online and all Martins, some Gibsons and a few other brands were all pulling in strong money. Surely that would be the business to be into if you could get them at the right price. You couldn't. And if you've read thus far you know where this is going. Being that you can't buy them and sell them on for much profit, I wonder if you could buy what looks like them, alter them slightly and then sell them on for profit? It turns out you can.

To start with I went online and bought up a few vintage guitars that looked like a Martin or a Gibson. Makes such as Ibanez and Takamine made models very similar, and back in the day they were very well made and sounded good. I had met a guy at work that could work wonders with wood – he'd come in to buy all the old pieces of furniture which he'd then break down and use this reclaimed wood to make new 'old' furniture, using the same old techniques and materials. He was a sweet old boy who was pulling small, innocent cons. I would have more than one venture with him (but we'll get to the other one later). He would go to antique furniture fairs and sell his 'finds'. He had a gift that he wasn't really using to his full potential and lots of time that could be better spent working with me. The offer he couldn't refuse was a set amount for each guitar he could make look identical to another; plus, all the free reclaimed wood he could get his greedy little hands on for his workshop. He agreed to take a look at what I had and said he would see what he could do. To start with I gave him a Gibson Hummingbird and a Martin D-28 from my own collection, plus two vintage Japanese copies, both Ibanez. They both had a similar look, sound and feel to the originals, the head stocks were clearly different with a different badge on all of them and with each having different inserts and stamps. But I'd got his attention and it was worth a punt.

My grandad had recently returned the guitar he gave to me all those years ago. Over the years in my possession it had got bashed around what with all the house moves and my general rock'n'roll lifestyle. He saw it in a sorry state and said he'd take it home to see if he could repair it. It came back looking brand new and my guilt for letting it get into such a sorry state was replaced with joy because of the great job he'd done in fixing it up. Now if my grandad could do that, I wonder what Ronnie could do with this lot. The possibilities are endless – or so I thought.

It wasn't long before the bubble burst because this wasn't going to be as straight forward as I had first perceived. Apart from the initial hurdle of Ronnie knowing absolutely fuck all about musical instruments, in particular guitars, i.e. how to play them, tune them, how the action should be, how they should and shouldn't sound etc – it turned out Ronnie knew as much about musical instruments as I did wood, nada, which made for a very challenging duo when it comes to partnering up in the business of selling iffy guitars. Not only that, but Ronnie would break the news to me that more than one material had been used. He started to mention spruce, cedar, rosewood, mahogany and maple. He went on the educate me further and tell me that the cheaper guitars were constructed using laminate. The name brands are expensive for a reason; which meant this operation was going to be very difficult, but not impossible to do. Needless to say, his price went up (classic tactics) and we re-negotiated. More guitars were bought to be stripped down and re-assembled, re-stamped, re-labelled, re-everything'd. I bought anything he asked for, scrap guitars, tuners, strings, hot coffee, biscuits and anything else. Eventually we started to make headway. The first couple were the hardest, most expensive and time consuming – but there's a first time for everything and after a while it started to work. A few weeks later and after what felt like a lifetime, Ronnie produced two 'Martin D-28s' and two 'Gibson Hummingbirds' from his workshop – two being

Mickey Mouse copies. They looked brilliant, a work of art, and the fact that I would have spent strong money on them and not know the difference, meant other idiots were going to do the same. And they did.

I ordered guitars on one online account and sold the finished articles on a different one. I changed my business account name to one that would lure the punters in. I was very careful with the wording of my advertisements and the buyer always had an option to return an item – which they never did. They were happy with their products, so was I and so was Ronnie. Everyone's a winner.

Online I was making a 1000% profit and after Ronnie's cut, I was still in it for good money. I wasn't ripping people off. I was just re-badging a product and moving it on. It's no different to car companies selling the exact same components with a different sticker on them and commanding ten-times the price, beauty products containing the same ingredients but calling it a different name and doing the same. So many of the multi-million-pound companies are doing it – it's all a con when you think about it.

Before long Ronnie and I were making good money with it all – me more so than him, but I was taking all the risk while he was the one with the workload. He was happy in his little shed defrauding the nation with his master carpentry and my hustler's ambition. Together we were a good team.

After a while Ronnie would fall ill, he was already almost deaf and the poor guy couldn't keep up with the workload plus I was getting bored. So again, as with all good things and like its predecessors this scam had to unfortunately come to an end. But it was good while it lasted – and Ronnie never ratted me out to anybody. God love him.

I later read that Gibson had actually taken Ibanez to court over their design copies, Ibanez, along with other guitar manufacturers were producing guitars that closely resembled other popular American models. The lawsuit between Ibanez and Gibson was eventually resolved in an out of court settlement – with Ibanez agreeing to change their designs on future models. This led to a change in how companies could approach their guitar designs, stopping direct copies with each one having to come up with their own, distinct design. It's thanks to them that we came up with the Ronnie Hummingbird and the Ronnie D-28.

CHAPTER 10

Convincing History

The Treasure Hoard Con

When I was a kid, I was obsessed with treasure. I had to keep a box with a lid on that I could close and lock. In it would be my most prized possessions. When I was really young it was my Thunderbirds collection and a few other knickknacks, buttons and costume jewellery, then as I got older the items would grow in value. Karl and I used to bury stuff in our gardens, being that we were neighbours. We used to imagine that we'd find them in 50 years' time when the world had changed drastically and our buried treasure would be worth a fortune, only to dig it all back up again at the end of the six weeks school holidays. I used to watch the Goonies and fantasize what it would be like to follow a treasure map and find Willie's treasure hidden somewhere that no-one else was lucky enough to ever come across. To be honest, not that much has changed really.

Another friend of mine, who wishes to remain silent in this escapade, so let's call him Del, would keep himself amused by going to the beach with some bits and pieces of costume jewellery and throw it out for the metal detectorists to find. He said it kept them busy and gave them a reason to get up in the morning. I quite liked this. Adding fuel to their fire and encouraging the dream to last a little longer – kind, harmless fun. This gave me an idea.

I took Del's seed and decided to pump it full of steroids and ramp it up a few notches. What if we buried actual treasure? Something for someone to find which was a big deal that would make the papers. That would be pretty cool. There were lots of snags with this idea though. What if it wasn't found at all? Or what if it was found but never reported? How would we know it had been found? And what would be the best thing to bury? Let's face it, if 100 people found a pot of gold how many people do you think would be honest enough to report it and hand it in? Not that many. I'll tell you now – I fucking wouldn't. I don't owe the world any favours and it certainly hasn't done me any. If it wasn't worth a small fortune and it was of particular and significant historical importance then yes, I may do then. But a pot of gold – get fucked. Finders' keepers.

So that was gold off the list, for now. The idea was left to simmer for a while then not too long after, a plan was hatched. What if an ancient hoard was discovered? Something had been missing for hundreds or even thousands of years, only to turn up on one fine metal detectorist's morning. That would certainly make someone's day, wouldn't it? I'd give anything to feel like what I imagine it would feel like for someone who spends their whole lives searching for this shit. It would be like winning the lottery in their world. So, we had the idea –

an ancient hoard. Next problem, where are we going to buy all this shit from? And what could we buy or make in the modern day that looks like it has been underground for eternity? Especially with today's technology, what with radiocarbon dating – this is something that was going to prove to be very difficult, but not impossible. We threw some ideas into the mix, wood, bones, coins, beads, stones, flint, leather, string, teeth, paper, slate. Should it be jewellery, weapons, money or manuscripts? At one point witchcraft and fucking spiritual dances were thrown into the mix. There was a lot to think about.

To begin with I got hold of a load of clay pots or vases – vessels if you will, to put the stuff into. This in itself proved to be a problem. Archaeologists will know the age of something just by the finish, base, colour, thickness and whether or not it has been wheel turned. In the end it was decided to get a few made up and give it a test run.

The very first one was going to be an ancient Chinese hoard. To go in the pot was going to be coins, some gold ingots, some jade, some hand carved wooden sculptures and whatever other shit we could throw in and get away with. First, the vase had to be sanded to make it look like it had been wherever it was found for God knows how many years. I dusted off the grinder and drill from the garage, and bearing in mind that masonry and pottery was not my forte, I got to work. Every edge needed to be sanded with odd, uneven scratches here and there, the scratches themselves had to be sanded so they didn't look fresh. The fragile pieces needed to be removed and the sharp edges worn down so they were smooth – like they had been rubbing against something for a long time.

In the end we got there, a few obliterated vases and a lung full or two of clay dust later and the finished article was produced. It didn't look too bad for a first effort. The neck of the vase was too small to fit the items we had come up with, unfortunately, but I couldn't wait any longer. Even with the knowledge that all rushed heists are destined for failure – I still wanted to push on so I cut off the base, crammed all the goodies into it then reattached it back on using a mixture of what materials I had lying around in the garage.

Next were the contents. I had been experimenting with a smelter that I'd bought on the internet with some scrap gold that I'd acquired. We wanted ingots or gold bars but didn't want to use genuine gold, not for a tester anyway so the next best thing we came up with to use was brass, which we did and they looked great, even stamped with a little Chinese symbol for good measure and polished to perfection. The hand-carved wooden sculpture was burned and sanded, soaked and dried, the jade sanded so it looked worn down, along with the other few bits. Next was where to put the fucking thing? If we buried it in the ground, it could be years until it is found. Plus, you need special permission to start digging up someone else's property, whether you're leaving treasure or finding it.

It was decided to stick with the beach, that way there are hundreds of people that would be walking over it every week with detectorists having full permission to detect without any hassle. We walked along the beach, decided roughly on where it should be placed then checked the tide times and the weather forecast. It needed to be on a dry day when the tide was out and preferably just as it started to get dark. We needed to time it right for when the beach was at its most empty so it couldn't be on a weekend. We had to be mindful of dog walkers, surfers, lifeguards and people going for a stroll. The day was chosen and the plan was put into action. So off we went, looking dodgy as fuck and about as subtle as a brick, we made our way onto the sand, fully wrapped up for winter carrying two shovels, an 'ancient' Chinese vase and two bags full of Chinese coins that we were also going to scatter for good measure. We counted out 100 steps offshore and kept in line with the second set of wooden stakes so we knew where our loot was – should we need to come back and retrieve it for some unknown reason.

Then we waited…and waited…and waited.

It was actually only a few weeks later when I got the call from Del but it felt like forever. 'Have you got your telly on, it's all over the fucking news?!' Yes, at fucking last. I put my TV on but nothing came up so I did a quick Google search and read the headlines: 'Police appeal after gold items found on the beach', it was already on the BBC news, viewed by over 74 million people in over 200 countries, then came Twitter and Facebook. Before we knew it there were people from all over commenting on what the items were, how old they were and why they'd been buried. The history buffs had got together, they were arguing back and forth but between them they had come up with their own conclusion, some differed but the majority had decided on the following: it was definitely a Chinese vase that had been buried as part of an ancient Chinese tradition. It was a ceremonial vase that was a gift for the afterlife and was between 675-725 years old. People were in uproar saying it shouldn't have been opened and that it should be put back where it was found. They were discussing the poor family's loved ones from 700 years ago and slating each other's points of view.

In the end they had to shut it down on Facebook and Twitter because it had stirred up a frenzy and people were going nuts. The police set up a hotline for anyone with any information to come forward in an effort to help with their investigation.

It's surprising what a cheap vase, some smelted brass, a few pendants, coins and some free gifts that belonged to your nan from a Chinese restaurant can really do to set off the perfect storm. And this was only the tester. I was hooked instantly.

It is amazing what people will come up with if you just plant the seed and let it grow and take its own direction. It never once crossed my mind about a Chinese death burial. It was just some Chinese-looking things in a vase. I simply thought they'd think it was treasure. It's an interesting sociological experiment to do something like this and see where it goes, and then watch from the sideline as the drama unfolds. The police report even said it was gold-coloured ingots, they never said anything about finding solid gold bars. The thing is people will believe what they want to believe, the same with most of the stuff I had sold. The 'sovereign' coin pendants, the 'signed' boxing gloves, the guitars. I never said that they were anything other than what they were, but people still paid good money for them.

I also find it interesting how a story will change as it is passed along. I know what was in that vase because I put it there, the police even put a photo up of the items that were inside it. That still didn't stop people from adding a bit to what they had heard before passing it on, and so on. By the time it had come back around to me the stories that I was hearing was that there were several kilos found, and of gold, not brass – one guy said they'd found £70,000 worth of gold bars, another said £140,000, it quickly snowballed. There were Chinese people coming forward with information as to what dynasty the contents had come from. It was fucking hilarious. And I needed to do more.

I had to be careful not to overdo it because it would seem a bit suspicious if all of sudden lots of hoards were turning up all over the shop, left, right and centre – but come on, this is me, and as with everything else I went over the top. Del thought it was funny too, we were egging each other on like two schoolboys and having a right laugh. He was buzzed after the news announcement and even bought a skull to go into the next find – he was talking about more black magic types of bizarre finds that would freak people out, whereas I was more into the hidden treasure.

I got another vase made up, exactly the same vase as the last time – so people would think they had come from the same place. This time, to go along with Del's requests, some bones were added for good measure. I had eaten a whole rack of ribs and thrown the bones into the garden for the cats to finish off. I retrieved the bones and cleaned them in bleach and vinegar then baked them in the oven to age them rapidly. The whole house fucking stank and I was glad when it was over. The combination of bleach and vinegar together alone isn't too good for you in an unventilated area – I know, I'd already witnessed that with the aging process of the Chinese coins in the last hoard.

The new one, the same as the last, was again taken to the beach. We chose a different spot this time, a bit further out to sea. Over the course of the week the sea had shifted the sand; it does this from time to time and exposes parts of shipwrecks from times past. It had exposed a kind of oil slick that was black and not very nice looking. Again, we scattered some extra coins about to get the detectorists' interest and made sure they were mainly around where we wanted to put the vase. That way when their beepers go off, they'd keep looking and soon be hot on the trail for the master prize we had waiting in store for them. I threw the sealed vase into a channel that was in the middle of the oil slick. To our amusement the fucking thing floated. It wasn't supposed to have done that; then again, we buried the last one. We quickly dug a hole, put the vase in and threw some sand on top of it. Del dug a few other shallow holes so it didn't look too obvious that people had been up to something in one place – as if kids had been playing with their buckets and spades, anything to cover our tracks. We left, and we waited, but not for very long.

A couple of days later on the off-chance, I went for a ride on my motorbike and thought I'd stop at the beach to do some intel. They were all at it. There was a metal detectorist up on the pebbles, there was one on the beach going up and down, and there was another one out by our oil slick. The guy out by the slick was plotting his movements with markers. He had covered about 50 metres with small squares and had his own little runway going so as to not cover the same area twice. You could see clear as day where he had been and where he still needed to investigate. The guy was definitely onto something. And no doubt he found what he was looking for – but all that followed thereafter was silence. The police had obviously shut down any reports and now were keeping things hush hush. There was no second Chinese vase reported, and I know for sure the guy found it – he was almost standing on the spot where we'd buried it a few days previous and he was right on the money, literally.

Unfortunately for us a spanner was thrown in the works because a few weeks later human body parts had been found washed up on the shore. Now this wasn't me, or Del – which is a good thing we hadn't buried that skull, could you fucking imagine what that would have been like?! What if we'd have been caught mid-burial and someone saw us getting rid of what was essentially a human skull? And then genuine human body parts had started to wash up on the shore. Try explaining that one to the judge. Lock them up and throw away the key. We'd have got life in prison, no questions asked.

Suffice to say, because of this Del seemed to lose interest in the operation and didn't seem to want any further involvement in the whole thing. He is a wise man, but I was just getting started.

Before long I had a bunch of new 'old' vessels loaded. We'd done two ancient Chinese hoards. I'd also got an ancient Greek hoard made up, an old English one and three from ancient Rome. The ancient Greek hoard was brilliant. I spent a long time getting this together. It had a manuscript, coins and weapons. I looked up some ancient Greek scripture and wrote a piece that had something along the lines of 'in order to have peace we must go to war'. I had arrow heads that were made from flint. This time the coins were genuine. They were tiny and I'd ordered lots of them. I'd got some thin lengths of leather and sanded them with sandpaper so they were worn. I then twisted the lengths into braids which I wasn't sure what I was going to use them for but had no doubt they would come in useful. I made a dagger from a large piece of flint and added a handle that was made from wood. I was worried the wood could be carbon dated but I was in a frenzy and my OCD wouldn't let me stop now. The braided leather did come in handy because I wrapped it tightly around the wooden handle and cemented it into place. I then saturated the whole dagger in bleach and acid, then baked it in the oven so it came out black, old, worn and definitely believable. I then put the whole lot into a vase that I had painstakingly prepared and sealed using wax, cork and cement. I then went and buried it next to the rocks and made note of exactly where it was so I could come back later and check the progress on whether it had been found or not.

Unfortunately, it was all for nothing – well, so far at least. I came back a few days later and the vase had been obliterated by the waves. They hit the rocks with some real force, enough to lift people off their feet and knock walls down, so the chances of anyone finding my clay pot in one piece were slim to none. It was a rookie mistake – I should've known really seeing as I'd nearly drowned in almost the same spot a few years previous. I searched everywhere and all I could find was one chunk of cement which had come from inside the vessel that had a coin stuck in it. I threw it back where I had found it in the hope that someone else would do the same.

As of yet I still haven't heard of anything, no comebacks and no police investigation. Maybe in a few years someone will find it. Keep your eyes peeled for any Ancient Greek/Neanderthal flint blades washing up on any shores around you. It's going to happen at some point.

And again, you heard it here first.

That one frustrated me because I had spent a lot of time and money on it, much more than the first two, and they took a while. I had spent days and nights working on it, researching it and getting everything just right. I was in the zone with it and couldn't stop myself. Getting so into it that I was again missing stops to eat because the time would fly past so quickly. By the time I realised it was nine o'clock at night and I'd gone without lunch and dinner.

I've always been this way, obsessive and on it – the kryptonite/ super power in full swing again.

After the Ancient Greek hoard, I carried out a few shit ones. The old English hoard wasn't much cop and was more of a giggle than anything else. That was just full of old English gold coins and put into an old clay beer bottle with a cork and slung into the river with not much imagination. I also did a Roman hoard – again without much imagination, it was just a vase that was sanded down with a load of replica coins put in this time and thrown out to sea – another one that will pop up in years to come, but nothing I'd want to have my name put to. I needed to up my game again.

Over the next few months, I decided to do some more research into Roman history and archaeological finds. I started ordering genuine Roman pottery, figurines, genuine coins from different time periods – I'd figured that if anyone was going to find the next hoard it was going to be big and the first thing they would do is get the coins fact-checked. If all the coins had been from different time periods, then the game would be up straight away. Those bastards ruled for hundreds of years so all the coins had to be perfect. I ordered rings for men and women, all genuine, other pieces of jewellery, animals that children would have played with. I was getting stuff sent over from America and it was getting out of hand – or it was getting good, depending on how you looked at it. If you're going to do something, then you may as well go big or go home and go for broke; but it was getting expensive. I had spent thousands upon thousands cooking up the perfect con trick and I'm not proud to say that I have ruined some perfectly good examples of fine Roman archaeological finds by smashing them in the process. Many cost me a small fortune, but they were for sale and I bought them, so they were mine to do with as I pleased. And it was only money. Fake stuff of value to trade with whatever I wanted in return for it.

I made more visits to the beach, each time with a few coins in my pocket, all Roman and all genuine. You can actually pick the coins up quite cheap online; it's getting them all from the right year that gets expensive. And the coins are tiny, much smaller than the replica shit you can buy, which I was unaware of at first. Every time I'd visit, I'd sling a few coins down, pretending I was bending down to pick up shells, which I did on occasion, then replacing the shell with a coin that I'd push into the wet sand.

I had to keep the detectorists interested, which they very much still were because I'd see them quite often as I went for a stroll. I even got someone to take a photo of me standing in front of some of them – unbeknownst to them that they were standing a few feet away from the culprit who was responsible for burying all this stuff in the first place. It did make me laugh though.

With Del well and truly out of the picture – which was unfortunate, but he knew I could be a bit obsessive and over the top and the body parts had done it for him and pushed him well out of his comfort zone – I still kept him in the loop and told him a few more things that I had up my sleeve, something which I very rarely do if I'm up to something. I have always preferred to work alone and keep things to myself. Somebody once told me that the only time three people can keep a secret is when two of them are dead. And he was right. For some reason people just can't seem to keep their mouths shut. They have to tell someone, even if it's one person. And then that person has to tell someone else, and so on. Then before you know it the whole fucking world knows and not only that, they have added their own two penn'orth to the story and now it is even bigger than it was before – just like the Chinese hoard. You can trust some people but they are very few and far between. And you can't trust different people with the same things. The same person I can trust with a secret I couldn't trust to give money to, to hold. And vice versa. People love drama, and they love a good story.

It didn't take long and the coins had all been deposited on the beach. Then I had a chance encounter at work. I was casually minding my own business when I noticed an old guy, who had been talking to one of my work colleagues, had a ring on. Being that I had my fair share of all things shiny I complimented him on it, telling him it was unusual and not what you normally see on a daily basis. It was gold, had some age to it and kind of masonic looking. He told me he had found it whilst metal detecting some years previous and my ears began to prick up as we struck up a conversation. I said I had been thinking about taking up metal detecting as a hobby but I didn't know how to get into it or what equipment I would need. He was a nice old guy and proceeded to give me a few handy tips on what to buy and where to go. I asked him if he had found anything interesting in the past, and lo and behold, he got his phone out and showed me his photo gallery of Roman finds he and his metal detecting buddies had acquired over the recent months. It was all there. They had found the very coins that we had placed on the beach in the few months leading up to the day, many Roman and quite a few Chinese. He told me to keep the information he was telling me quiet, so I knew something was definitely up with regards to the Police. He said it seemed strange because he had been detecting that area for years and had never found anything like it before. He didn't understand why all of a sudden, the contents of ancient Rome were flooding the beaches nearby. I casually said that they must have come from somewhere, then added maybe they all came from the same place, sewing the seed that maybe they were all once in one big container of sorts – to which he agreed, but said they hadn't found any pottery. That was it, alarm bells ringing – I needed to get another pot, and fast. I said my goodbyes; I liked him, and I didn't feel bad. He was quite excited as he was telling me all about his treasure and how it was enough to constitute a hoard, being that there was so much of it – he'd already been in touch with the relevant authorities. I went home and spent the evening searching for the ideal vessel.

Eventually I got hold of what I was looking for, did my usual workshop activities in the garage and a few more lungfuls of clay dust later and it was ready. One very large Roman pot, big enough for 5,000 Roman coins. I put some coins in it along with some period-correct spearheads and this time left it with no lid on; it had to look like all the previous coins had come from it. I trotted off to the beach once more and found the perfect spot where it wouldn't be smashed to smithereens like the Greek hoard some months prior. I had to keep drip feeding this adventure, because one day soon it would all make sense. Plotting from different angles and popping up here and there with another little piece for the puzzle – all roads lead to Rome eventually, and it was going to be awesome. I left it 'stuck' between some driftwood from an old tree and put some seaweed over it for good measure – ready for the appropriate agent to stumble across.

I'd been scouting about on eBay and elsewhere online looking for the perfect vessel for another one, the big one – the finale. I didn't want this one to be very big in size because this time I had to be as covert as possible because where it was going was likely going to be accompanied with many beady eyes. It would look a bit strange if one guy on his own was seen with a large pot in one hand and a spade in the other. They were each going to have to fit in my large coat pockets. I was going it alone now and had been for a while and it had to be perfect. I didn't want there to be any possibility of error. I found a suitable pot and this time it was made of bronze. It had great patina which is hard to replicate. A lot of things that are artificially aged are easy to spot under close scrutiny, if not by the naked eye, then definitely under microscope and scientific reporting. Plus, a bronze vessel isn't going to break, maybe I should have thought about this before but I was less knowledgeable about what the Romans got up to when I had got started in all of this. I didn't even know they had bronze jugs.

I wanted the coins to be perfect as well. I had found some online but the majority of them were from one seller, they were only being sold in singles and he wasn't up for selling in bulk at a reduced price like some others. They were in fairly good nick, which they needed to be as I wanted the finder to think they had been unmolested for the past 2000 years. They, again, had to all be from the same time period, so gradually I started ordering them at £20-£30 a time.

The vessel itself had already cost me over £600 and that was before customs and postage charges, so I was going to be in it for a fair amount of money when I had finally got everything I needed.

I also wanted more than just coins so set about looking for some jewellery to go in the pot as well. I had used rings before, both men's and women's, but these had to be something a bit special, like they were loved by someone and look as though a lot of work had gone into them in a period where tools and manufacture wasn't up to the standards that we have today. I knew they were limited back in the day with what stones they could use in their rings.

Diamonds were very rare back then and they didn't have the tools or skills to cut and polish them. Only the super-rich and powerful would have had them and they would have been rough, even then, and look just as they were found in the ground. The same with rubies, emeralds and sapphires. What if I made them? I had smelted metals before and that way they would look like they were created with limited means – like the limits of my workshop for example. In the end I'd got what I set out to achieve, a man and woman's ring, very pretty, gold with a red stone. I bought some others online that I'd add to the collection, I wanted this hoard to be of great interest and something to get people talking.

I needed some arrowheads as well. I'd bought them before but these had to be a bit special as well. The others I had bought were rusty and in bad condition. These had to be good enough to stick straight back on the arrow and fire at the enemy – I found some. I wanted some kind of beads, but had to be careful not to include anything the same as I had used before because as soon as they're sent off to be verified, people would start asking questions.

I hit upon the idea of semi-precious shells. They were pretty and would work alongside the rings quite well. As if they belonged to people who had some money but weren't rich – middle class if you like. I came across some old bone dice as well and they were great to use because of their size; so, they were thrown into the mix. Then some figurines and some toys. I ordered a collection of them from a buyer who claimed they were bought direct from an archaeologist. As soon as they turned up, I knew they were bullshit. You can't scam a scammer! Well, you can, you just have to be a better scammer than the person you are scamming. They looked okay to the untrained eye, but one of the items in the collection was way off. It was far too intricate for the production methods of the time. I messaged the seller and said I'd had them checked out by my scientific team and that their conclusions were that they were modern replicas made to look old. I was met with sincere apologies and the blame was put on the 'archaeologists that had sold them' to him. That old chestnut. Blame shifting red flag no2. I wasn't annoyed, it quite amuses me when people try it on. Another seller with 100% feedback and thousands of positive feedback reports. Cheeky bugger. Nice try.

I would need to keep looking for some figurines but as soon as I got them, I was almost good to go. Now I had to think of the exact place to put my hoard. I had the same problem as before – it had to definitely be found, and the finder needed permission to find it. How could I trust that the finder was going to be honest and tell the authorities what they had come across? I needed to know 100% when it was going to be found and by whom. Luckily enough I already had these answers. I knew for sure when and where it would all take place. You want to know how I knew all of this?

Because the finder was going to be me.

Do you know how much museums are willing to pay for genuine hoards discovered throughout England? A fucking arm and a leg, that's how much. And I had the winning lottery ticket. Everything else had been part of the build up to the grand finale. I didn't look at the thousands I had spent as wasted money. It was money I had invested. I looked at it like I was earning whilst I was learning, like the interest you earn as you start saving in a bank. I was putting money in, but I would be taking it all back out again, and then some.

So where was it going to be discovered? I had exhausted the possibilities of anywhere local to me because hoards would be turning up all over the shop. This had to be something a bit further afield. I researched all the hoards that had been discovered in England and decided it was going to be in one of those places. I looked up what coins, etc had been found and matched it to the timeframe that I had in my collection. I picked one that ticked all the boxes but it was going to be a while away. And when I discovered my find what was I going to tell the authorities was the reason for even being there in the first place? I came up with the perfect excuse, my vessel was packed and I was ready for the off.

In the meantime, the big jug that was capable of holding 5,000 coins with the arrowheads/coins in had been discovered. A woman who had been holidaying in Devon with her husband had stumbled across a large 'Roman' pot that was 'nestled' in a large piece of driftwood. She took to social media to publicise her findings and before long someone had uploaded her TikTok video to Facebook. Then came the comments. In much the same way as the Chinese hoard sometime previous, everybody came flooding in with their 'expert' advice. Some were calling her a fraud, saying she had made the video for likes, and others were amazed with her discovery. In the video she told the viewers that she had reported her find to the relevant authorities and was waiting for them to get back to her. Then came a second video answering some of the questions that had been put forward by the interested parties. Again, this brought a smile to my face as she was super excited about what she had found. I tagged Del in the video who was still watching from the sidelines and we had a chuckle about how much money she would be getting from the museum offer. As of yet there haven't been any updates. Good luck to her. I never did 'find' that last hoard. That's not to say it wasn't buried. Good luck. I'm retired.

El Ultimo Tesoro

March forward like the cavaliers and roundheads,
Look east where artillery lies.
Little white towns have many 'o' places,
We remember them from days gone by.
They came 1st century AD,
And again, thirty-nine, forty-five.
By land, by sea, and by river,
Land Ho, twenty-first, twenty-five.
Under rocks and grains, you should seek some,
Near driftwood, the slip, under stars.
The greatest guns shall protect one,
By hook or by crook they're not far.

CHAPTER 11

Was It Just Breakfast?

The Tiffany Con

I carried on dabbling in the jewellery game. If DeBeers and all those other diamond companies can make a lot of money by manipulating every bride and groom to be on planet earth then there was definitely a way that I could get into some of that action. If people were happy enough and more than willing to part with vast sums of money as I've said before, then I'd like to help relieve them of some of it.

DeBeers had men over a barrel. And it was brilliant. Instead of selling the diamonds to the men, they did something different. They went through their wallets through their women. They sold an idea that a man's love would be measured by the size of the diamond he can afford. The bigger the diamond, the more the cost= the greater the love. And almost every woman wants a sparkly jewel to show off to her friends. It's status. And almost every man wants to please his lady – if he doesn't, his life wouldn't be worth living. She would let him know that he is a loser and remind him of that fact for the rest of his days. So, what does he do? He goes out and buys the biggest diamond he can afford, which is more than he can afford. Because he loves her, he likes sex and he wants a quiet life, plus – he wants her to say yes. And if he can't quite afford it, then that's what credit cards are for, right? Now he spends the next few years paying it back, and then some. Do you think DeBeers gives a shit about all that? Do they fuck. It's three months' salary, now pay up! And people do. Thousands and thousands for a polished transparent stone on a metal band. It still amazes me.

With the advent of HPHT and CVD lab-grown diamonds the cost of owning a diamond has come down, but their prices are still fucking high. And because the market has been flooded with them it has brought the value of mined diamonds down.

At one time DeBeers controlled the majority of the market. They could decide how many stones they would release onto the market. By controlling the supply and demand means you can predict and command the price you want, i.e. their value. As we have already said, the rarer something is the more it is worth. Which is shame because I have an almost flawless 3.00 carat oval diamond ring at home. A few years ago, it was probably worth double what I could get for it now. But it's all relative bullshit. It cost me next to nothing, so relatively speaking, I haven't lost a penny. And I don't even wear it. The same with my watch.

Through all of my childhood and my teens I wanted a 'prestigious' wristwatch. It would mean I had made it, that I had become someone and something. That Rolex I switched at the pawn shop made me feel like a king, for about five minutes. It's like a lot of things. You want something so bad then when you finally have it it's not like what you thought it would be. At the time I thought it was because I had stolen it that it didn't feel as good as it should have done. I told myself that if I'd bought a watch with 'hard-earned' money that I didn't make from any scams then it would feel completely different.

So, through the job I was working at I saved up and bought myself a gold Omega Seamaster. Again, I felt like a king – but not for very long. I was still me but with a shiny new watch and it didn't mean anything. I'm sat here now with a Casio G-Shock strapped to my wrist. It looks like something you used to get back in the 80s. My son tells me they have come back into fashion. I bought it because it is solar powered, and it tells the time and date.

In my life I have owned several wristwatches of the connoisseur's variety. Apart from the Cartier as a kid that mysteriously went missing and the Rolex.

In order of rags to riches (as I started early when I didn't have much money, but still had an obsession with watches) I have had two stainless steel Omega Seamasters, a gold Omega Seamaster, a Breitling Colt 36, a gold and stainless steel Breitling WindRider automatic, A Breitling SuperOcean 44 (by now I'd fully realised it was all bullshit…), and finally the Breitling B1 Professional – which I still feel is the best model Breitling ever produced, and one of the cheapest I've owned. That being said, none of them was much over £5,000. Thankfully, I realised the absurdity before it reached greater heights.

I can't believe, well I can, that people wear timepieces, and that's all they are – a tool to tell the time – on their wrists that cost hundreds of thousands of pounds, sometimes a million or more. In saying that, it's normally by the super-rich that have realised that money isn't real and that's it's only the poor who believe that it is. The only time my flash watch and diamond ring come out of the safe now is to impress some other idiots who think they're impressive. They're good for business meetings, picking up gold-diggers and advertising that you want to get robbed. Other than that, they're useless, apart from one tells the time of course. Unless you trade in watches, then they are useful.

I couldn't believe how much the Rolex Daytona's were going for on the second-hand market. More than they fucking cost in the first place.

I'd like to be a fly on the wall when these women go into the jeweller to re-sell their engagement rings that cost their ex-husbands their life savings – only to be told that it is worth 1/10th of the price that was paid for it in the first place. The reality is no lady wants to wear something that has come from a failed marriage! The best that can be done is to rip out the stone, melt the gold or the platinum and then re-set it into a fresh mount, throw it in a box and sell it on for ten times to the second-hand purchase price. How much is his love worth to you now, lady? Fuck all.

In 2024 Tiffany & Co sold a diamond engagement ring through Sotheby's for 5.3 million – I hope she was special. I wonder what she'd get back for that when she takes it into the pawn shop. I took a 7.5 carat diamond tennis bracelet into a jeweller once to see how much they'd offer me for it. I had no intention of selling it, I just wanted to see what the fuckers were going to say to me. I went in with jeans and a sweatshirt, looking as casual as I could to give the impression I didn't know much about jewellery. The lady looked it over, asked where I'd got it and why I was selling it before offering to hand over £200. Two hundred fucking quid. The gold content alone was worth a lot more than that. I told her this then left the shop abruptly as she hastily followed me throwing out a few more offers as I left the building. I've done this on a few occasions. I had to go and get a load of jewellery valued in order to get them covered by contents insurance with the house – I would have done it myself but it had to be from a legitimate jeweller. Just for a giggle I took in a 5.5-ounce solid gold chain, some other diamond tennis bracelets, a 3.00 carat diamond ring with the finest of stones, and some heavy solid gold pendants, and asked what I could get for them. Again, I made out I was none the wiser, and that I needed to raise money as I had lost my wife and home, it was all bullshit but I was curious. I wanted to punch the bitch in the face when she offered me less than a quarter of what it was all worth in just gold scrap value alone on that particular day, and that was without the stones.

That is a scoundrel right there. And they get away with it. I like to see their faces when you then start to talk about gold, their scrap value, how much it is that day and how much to the gram that everything weighs, the cut, colour, carat and clarity of the diamonds and what the hallmarks mean on each piece. It's quite satisfying to watch them sink into their chairs, knowing that you know that they have just tried to screw you. It may sound rich coming from a guy who is writing a book about a con artist who the authorities couldn't catch, but I did it in a different way. I re-badged things I was selling but they were still getting a good product.

There was one scam that I hated myself for which remains the only con I have ever regretted, but once I'd started it and got in too deep there was no going back. And since then, I've never repeated it. It wasn't that big of a con either, it was still in the thousands but it went against everything I believe in and I've never done it again. We'll get into that later.

Where were we? Oh yes, diamonds and stupid people. Selling to rappers, that would've been a good market to get into. They are largely clueless about jewellery, have money to burn, come from nothing and feel a sense of worth sporting the polished rocks. Maybe that's something that could have worked? Anyway, Tiffany. I'd noticed when walking through town whilst doing my obsessive magpie shop window routine that prices of diamond rings jumped up a hell of a lot as soon as a top brand was put under the ring in the display case. 1.00 carat rings were going for thousands. Some would argue 'yes, but it's a prestigious brand and look at the colour and the clarity'. Bullshit – it's all bullshit. The name is a name and some of the stones I saw were terrible. This did give me an idea though. I'd tried going straight with my diamond ring enterprise before and struggled to shift the goods on. And they were awesome rings with great stones. I'd had a great product but they weren't selling. I went and looked online and even second-hand Tiffany rings were commanding high prices. They were asking for much more than the rings I had been selling – and these were pre-owned. That's what I was missing, a name, a gimmick, another farce that people buy into. It's just another desperate attempt to show those around you that you have money. Look what this says, and I can afford it.

I decided to give it another try, but this time not so straight and above board. I'd tried that before and it didn't work. Sometimes you have to work twice as hard when it's legit. Fuck that. I was still going to be selling a great product, and the great British public was still going to be getting their deal of a lifetime, but it was going to be done a little different. I was going to sell Tiffany diamond engagement rings but replacing them with my own stones. Borrowing their name if you will to sell on my product. How hard could it be? Buy a second-hand ring, rip the stone out, replace it with a fat chunky new bobby dazzler, clean it, polish it, throw in a box, add a certificate and Bob's your uncle. The soon-to-be missus gets a new ring with a ridiculously high valuation that she tells all her friends about, the boyfriend gets an awesome blow job and a happy fiancée plus a few grand saved, and I get a wallet full of cash. It made perfect sense. But like most other get rich quick schemes and scams, it wasn't going to be without its own set of challenges.

I went online to look at making a start with purchasing the Tiffany bands. It didn't matter how small the diamond was because they would be surplus to requirements.

Pretty much straight away I noticed that the stamps and hallmarks differed depending on what year the ring had been produced. Not only that, each modern stone is laser etched with a serial number that corresponds to the certificate that comes with each purchase. It would appear that I wasn't the first cheeky devil to be coming up with such antics. But where there's a will, there's a way, this was a slight bump in the road and I soldiered on. All it meant was I would have to be selling rings that came out pre-2004 and I figured it's metal, stones, paper and a box. Who cares? And I was right – almost no-one.

Before long I had a box of bands ready to go. I had been wheeling and dealing for weeks to get them for the right price. Haggling the prices down with the usual bartering bullshit. 'It's scratched, there's no paperwork with it, it doesn't come with a box, it's the wrong size, it's worn, it's tarnished, the claws need repairing, the stone has an inclusion, it's old, it's bent, it's absolutely anything to get the price down a bit'. It doesn't matter how much money I have, I still need to get a bargain.

I think I get this from my nan. She could wear a diamond cocktail necklace with some matching earrings she bought from a charity shop. Or shoes that she bought for 500 euros with a skirt that cost two. We all love a bargain. The bands had to also pre-date when Tiffany had started putting the carat size on the inside of their bands, 0.19, 0.25, 0.55, etc. There was a way around everything. I was buying pre-owned anyway to save money and a lot of them were before then. I even bought the certificates straight off the internet. I was going to produce my own then found a seller who you could buy certificates from that were already made up, they were left blank where it said cut, colour, carat and clarity so you could just fill in whatever you wanted with an old type writer that I had got from work. I bought the diamonds in loose from abroad and found dealers who were reliable, fast and willing to do deals if I bought wholesale. I wanted to stay around the 1.00 carat mark. There's something about a 1.00 carat stone that gets people excited. For anyone with a bit of cash to flash, the 1 carat stone seems to be the magic number, not too big, not too small – and the price of them very much reflects this. Just search online and look at the price difference between a 0.95ct loose diamond and one that is 1.01cts. Sometimes you can pay double. I'll take the 0.95ct thanks. It can look exactly the same size to the naked eye and depending on the cut – if the stone has a good spread, then you can get plenty of bang for your buck. I bought a 0.37ct oval brilliant cut diamond once. The table and crown of the stone (the top surface and upper edge which you see from a bird's eye view) was massive but the stone was very shallow. Once set in a ring it looked the same size as another diamond that was 1.02cts! That's because the latter was so deeply cut. From the side it was noticeable but from the top they looked the same.

There are lots of tricks in the trade and a few optical illusions, like using a yellow gold mount for a 'warm' (slightly yellow) stone, the colour of the yellow gold band gives the illusion that the stone is whiter, the same with setting a warm stone IN a mount as opposed to on top of it, it would, again, make the stone appear whiter than it actually is.

I bulk bought hundreds of these stones in sometime prior, a few at first, then when I could trust the supplier, my orders increased. I got the stones set into new heads and had them re-set onto the rings. Some were easy, some were finnicky. Occasionally I had to get new shoulders put onto them and sometimes it was straightforward. Every now and then it was just a case of opening up the prongs or claws and replacing the diamond, but this was very rare as nearly all of them were being replaced with much larger stones. I stuck to gold as well, and only yellow, no white gold and no platinum. Once set the rings would be highly polished to perfection to look as if brand new. I bulk bought Tiffany boxes which you can purchase in the dozens. There are a lot of fakes floating around (cheeky monkeys), but if you look at the colour you can usually tell the fakes from the genuine. Failing that, if you hold the box up to the light or feel the material with light fingers you can feel the difference. They're difficult to tell on their own but easy when you have both the genuine and the fake side by side. So that was it and the operation was ready for the off. Diamonds ordered, bands ordered, boxes ordered, certificates ordered and completed, stones set, polished and ready. Now all that had to be done was sell them.

I checked out online what others were selling for (of the same or very similar cut, colour, carat, clarity and metal purity) and took off 33%. This was a good price – if you list too low people instantly start asking questions, if you price too high then nobody is interested. But -33%, and everyone wants to jump in and get a bargain. They sold like hot cakes and I couldn't get the gold bands in quick enough. Everyone seemed to be at it. It's surprising how much people don't know about jewellery, diamonds and engagement rings. That, plus the fact they actually just don't care. If they are getting something for a good price then that's all they care about. Some of the shitshows that I saw on people's fingers at the jewellers that I was working in were terrible, and these people were showing them off. They were showing me with a smile and asked what I thought about them – then I had to awkwardly say 'yes, that's lovely', whilst secretly wondering why this lady was showing off a shiny turd that she had been presented with.

It brings a smile to my face knowing there are hundreds of women out there sporting my diamonds and will be wearing them for the next 50 years or more. Well, that's the 50% that go the distance – another con, but anyway. I can sleep at night because I know what they have is genuine and a lot better than most of the other shit you can buy. They got a big, clear stone and their husbands got a bargain.

In the end I was running out of bands to buy and had sucked the internet dry. But more so than that. I got bored. My OCD had run its course and I wanted to move onto the next dream – just like the films when I was a kid. The next big thing, the next scam, the next hit of dopamine and adrenaline. Onwards and upwards.

CHAPTER 12

Pulled Chains

The Antiques Con

I've been interested in antiques for as long as I can remember. I'd much prefer to have a house full of oldy-woldy things as opposed to modern poorly made, mass-produced rubbish. Internally I pull a face of disgust every time I see a piece of furniture that has been made from chipboard. I hate the weak, cheap and good-for-nothing (other than burning), load of shit – and even that is a struggle for it.

If I was poor, I wouldn't use it, I'd instead have a piece of pine or any other solid wood that was bought from the tip, which I have done before, and still do. You can still get good quality for less. I like antiques because they remind me of an antique era, not that I have even lived in an antique era, not yet, but I like anything to do with history and bygone times.

When I was a kid my friend's dad had a shop selling antiques. One day someone burned it down; looking back it was most probably an insurance job but me and my friend Toby still went back to have a look around after it had been condemned and taped off. We had to be careful and make sure we kept to the edges so we didn't fall through the floorboards. There was still stuff in there like silver spoons and other bits and pieces.

We had a massive antiques store in our home town when I was growing up. It had three floors and had everything in it, anything you could think of. I thought it was the best place in the world and went in there any chance I could. I used to look through the glass and stare at the old pistols and semi-automatics in the display case – vowing to myself that one day I would have one – something I would make come true a few years later. It had gold jewellery and silver utensils for all occasions, old medals, China, swords, clothes and trinkets – a magnificent place. It's not there anymore, another place closed to make way for Turkish barbers and cash-only car washes.

We used to get loads of antiques in at work all the time. Back then people didn't have camera phones or the internet so they couldn't take photos of everything, then scan it through the internet and know how much something was worth in an instant. During my time in that job I have seen almost everything come in, from all different eras, some things worth an absolute fortune, and some things not so valuable, but still very interesting and from all over the globe. One day a trailer came in with two guys that were doing a house clearance. Strapped to the back is what can only be described as Tutankhamun's tomb. It was like Howard Carter had emptied it straight onto the trailer and brought it back for me. When it came in our customers were all over it like a rash. I managed to get in quick and swiped King Tut's death mask for myself. I hid it out the back then re-purposed it later.

I had a whole lock-up full of this type of stuff that I was collecting for I don't know what. My wife at the time didn't feel the same way about it all as I did. She thought it was old shit, while I viewed it all as long-lost treasure. She was more into the chipboard shit I mentioned earlier. When we split up, I had to move in with a relative so unfortunately the whole lot had to go. I didn't know what to do with it all at the time so loaded up a van a bunch of times and took the whole lot to an auction house where I was ripped off immensely.

Funnily enough, a few months ago I saw the very same King Tut death mask listed on eBay. It had made its way abroad and it was selling for a lot of money. I tried to get it back but the seller was asking for thousands, and being that I remember how much I got for it originally there was no way I was going to give him that – folded paper or not. I will get another one day, but it will have to be something a bit special to match what I had – but it will happen.

One thing I have always been interested in is apothecary cabinets, bottles and boxes. It probably has something to do with my life-long interest in drugs – or remedies if you will. Not that I partake in such devilish things these days, but for a long time they were my magic potions and cure for anything. I especially like the Victorian era so when something of that nature ever came in, I had to grab it. Someone threw an old apothecary cabinet into the skip. The drawers were great but the carcass had been damaged beyond repair. Ronnie (the wood guy) saw me rescuing it from the skip and asked me what I was doing with it. He was eyeing it up for himself but there was no chance. We got talking and like before he told me about some of the repair work he'd been doing for people. I asked him if he could fix it up for me which he agreed to – for a price. A couple of weeks later he phoned me up and told me it was ready and to come and collect. I took my van down to pick it up and he invited me into his lock-up to grab the unit. He had every type of wood there is and ever was and everything was old and all different lengths and thicknesses. On his worktops he had part-finished projects he was working on to sell on. My cabinet looked as though it had just rolled out of the workshop in Victorian England.

It was beautiful, freshly stained but not over the top, with each drawer fitting perfectly. Luckily it had retained its original ivory knobs which were still in great condition. I took it home and was made up, I got hold of some antique labels, each a different name of a drug or potion from back in the day and it suited the cabinet perfectly. That piece is another of my great regrets and something I wish I had back again – but needs must at the time and in a panic, I sold it because I didn't have the space.

Upon seeing what Ronnie had been up to again I wanted in on the action. I had seen what he could do and from the information I gathered he was still only doing his gig on very small proportions and was missing out on some decent paydays. He was selling maybe one piece of furniture every month or so and he couldn't envision a way to make it any bigger. I let him know of my ability in being able to sell sand to the Arabs and fridges to Eskimos, I had a means to store items, transport items, and a platform to sell them on. We would be reaching thousands of people and not just 50 or so. The idea was small and simple but it didn't stay that way for long.

It was to get all the antique furniture in from work through me, for free, then store it in my lock-up, one piece on top of the other in stacks of two, three or four, depending on how big each piece was. Then two pieces at a time would be taken to Ronnie's workshop where he would fix them up and make them look kosher again. Then when they were tarted up, I would advertise them, flog them and deliver them for some extortionate sum and we would both be quids in, which we started doing and the money started to roll in. It was honest, fairly easy but dull. Then something happened that would change all that in a flash. One day someone threw an old apothecary box into the skip. It was from the 1800s, it was missing its utensils, but it was mostly there. I asked Ronnie if he could fix it up for me whilst I searched the internet for the missing items. He repaired it within a week, I'd replaced the contents within two, and within three I would've had £2,000 sitting in the bank. What the fuck happened there? That was easy. Hmm…I was about to hit accept on the offer that I had received when I hit upon an idea. What if we could replicate what I had just almost sold??? I asked Ronnie and he said yes, no problem, other than finding the right period correct fixings. Why the fuck hadn't he thought of this before? Apothecary boxes were small, lightweight and could be sent in the post. What the fuck was he doing messing about at antique fairs with large units when the whole time he could have been making and selling these little gold mines?! I have noticed over the years that with a lot of people the answers to their problems are staring them right in the face sometimes. 'There's none so blind as those who will not see' I think is the expression. So, using the first apothecary box as the template and plans to go from, and just like the guitars, Ronnie was put to work. He had a knack for making something look the spitting image of something else. He lived and breathed wood, devoted his life to it – but was still poor. I would help to change that, twice, for as long as we could make it last.

They looked great, there were lots of little drawers and hidey holes for all the potions and apparatus, secret compartments in all different sizes for the travelling chemist of yesteryear. I bought in hundreds of bottles but it wasn't a chore for me and I got right into it. Ronnie needed me at the beginning and the end, and I needed him in the middle. I bought in labels and stuck them to the bottles, making sure they looked old and worn and not too perfect.

This con would unfortunately be short-lived. The main problem with our product was that we were creating a rare piece in large quantities. There's only so much of the same thing that you can sell at antique fairs, through friends of friends, marketplace and online. People were soon to start asking questions.

It did seem a bit odd that we seemed to have the exact same apothecary boxes containing all the bottles, keys, devices and labels, time after time, week in, week out. The product was great, the execution was brilliant, but the idea was flawed. We sold a few dozen, and some went for around the £2000 price tag. It was time to shut up shop and have a re-think. I'd made some money and Ronnie was eating steak. But it had come to an end.

CHAPTER 13

Ever Question Government?

The Big Fish Con

In order to be a successful conman, you must be able to lie and manipulate. I learned from my parents how to do it. The first lie I ever told was to my father. I'd been playing with my toy model aeroplanes that I'd got from the dump. They were old Airfix model kits that someone had built some years previous and thrown them away. They were old and tatty-looking but it added to their character and I loved them. My favourite was the Lancaster bomber, it had windows that you could see into the cockpit and it was very detailed, right down to the controls. I had been playing with my brother and accidentally stepped on one of his toys and broke it. He started crying and when my dad asked what the problem was, my brother said it was because one of his toys was broken. My dad saw me playing with the planes and, as a punishment, asked which one was my favourite and told me that if I was going to break my brother's toys then he was going to break mine. I wasn't stupid enough to answer him back and tell him that it was an accident, so instead I did something different. I knew my dad meant what he said and I knew what was coming next so I told him that my favourite was the Spitfire. He smashed it to pieces right there in front of me – but the Lancaster was safe.

My dad was a good guy but he had a mean streak. If he got angry, he would break stuff. He did the same to my go-kart that my grandad had built for me from my old pram I had as a baby, all because he'd come home in a mood and my mum had given him an ear-full. I'd kept that go-kart for years and it was well-made, but it didn't stand a chance when my dad was on one.

My mum would shout and scream but she wasn't physically scary like my father. Trying to batter us with whatever came to hand never worked because she was too weak. Her greatest weapon was my dad. If we did something wrong then all she would have to do was tell him and then we were fucked.

If my brother and I were bad then we'd get it when he got home from work. The method of discipline and order of things went a bit like this. He'd ask us which one wanted it first – which inevitably was me (I always figured I'd get in first and get it out the way). Then he'd line us up and tell us to turn around. After me it was my brother's turn, and after the double bubble we'd then cry and get sent to our rooms where we'd compare the marks left by our father. And to finish things off nicely, my mother would ask us to show her the marks, she would then reprimand our dad for hitting us too hard, she'd make us show him the marks, and he'd apologize. And the process was over with until the next time. Cheers, Ma – you could've just not grassed us up to begin with.

My mum used to stick up for me when I was a very young boy. Those flashbacks I mentioned at the beginning are of pissy mattresses, itchy legs and her screaming at my dad because of how he was with me and to stop because I was too little. My sister for the most part was left alone because she was a girl. She would still witness the arguing and I would try and take her away from it when she was a toddler. She too, has some scars, some I'm sure she isn't even aware of.

As I said earlier my dad did a lot of things right, but he got a few things wrong. It was him that took me to the dump in the first place, and it was him that bought me the planes. He had the power over us, and my mother had the power over him.

I used to watch my mother a lot when I was young which is something I didn't really do with my dad. How she would operate and how she spoke to people. I noticed from a very young age how she would speak to others when they were with her and how differently she spoke about them when they had gone. I found it very confusing why adults were nice to each other's faces but scolded each other when they weren't there.

Some women, I have come to learn, have to adapt to wicked cruelty in order to win. For the most part they don't have the ability to win an argument by physical force, so they win their battles by means of manipulation. It's very clever, a bit sick, and a bit twisted – but it's common. My dad was hands-on, too forceful, and it hurt when he beat the shit out of you – but he wasn't twisted. I'd choose a whack any day over a mind-fuck.

If my mother ever wanted anything she would get it by means of manipulation. She was very cunning when she wanted to be and would do this to get what she wanted. Since entering her sixties, she has seemed to have turned a corner and has been more 'mum'-like. I have welcomed this but with caution because I'm not used to it and it feels strange.

I have enjoyed having a mum for the last year and a half or so; part of me thinks it's because she has realised what's more important in life, and the other thinks that she's at a time in her life where she is lonely, the men in her life have gone, she knows she's getting old and will need looking after one day. They say leopards and spots, we'll see. She never read to us when we were kids, she never kissed us good night, we were never hugged as children and we were never told that we were loved. Ever. If it wasn't for my nan I would have definitely been in prison or a mental home long before now. I had my nan; my sister had our other nan; and my brother had a bit of both. Thank fuck the drugs and alcohol kept me sane – for a while.

I feel like I lost my mother at age five, the same way you do with your parents when you're a child in a supermarket. You walk around in relative peace because you know they are there, then all of a sudden you turn around and they're gone – and you panic. Suddenly you're in the big wide world all on your own and have to fend for yourself. She left when I was five, and re-appeared when I turned 40.

Better late than never.

I was 15 when I found out my father wasn't biologically related to me. It came out just before my final exams at secondary school, which was impeccable timing. I always knew I was different but just looked at it as I took after my mother – with my brother and sister taking after our dad. It made sense why my brother was always under the bonnet of a car with my dad and why I was always out with my friends. Now I know why he looked at me the way he did sometimes. No doubt I reminded him of someone else, especially as I started to grow older – which is the reason I could see the hatred in his eyes. I know my dad loved me very much but it wasn't enough to not screw me up. Who was I and where did I come from? Who did I come from? Who did I take after? Off the rails time, copious amounts of drugs time.

It wasn't just that the man I'd been calling Dad for all these years technically wasn't, it was also that half of my family who I had been calling family for, for all these years, who all knew about this lie, everyone except me, biologically wasn't.

Not only that but there was another family out there that WAS biologically related to me, and they knew, but where the fuck were they? I had a brother out there, cousins, aunties, uncles and grandparents who'd I never met. What the actual fuck? Take more drugs, make it go away.

I received a letter in the post once. With it was a photo of my biological father. It was of him holding me as a baby. He had the same hands and face as me and his eyes were my own. It was like looking at a shorter version of me at the same age. Very strange.

Everyone has a different story about what happened way back when. I don't know if it will ever be resolved. Maybe one day I will meet him. I do feel a strong sense of loyalty to my father for bringing me up for all those years. When the truth came out my dad sat with me and told me that when he met my mum my biological father didn't want anything to do with me. He said he went round to see him and was told that my mum was just a fuck. I don't believe that. It was wrong of him to be saying those sorts of things to me, but he had tears in his eyes as he was talking. I think it was just something he said out of anger and sadness and maybe fear – thinking I'd run off to find some long lost relative. My nan told me that none of this was true and that he thought he was doing the best by me. She said he would go round to visit her and ask to look at photos of me as I was growing up.

I've listened to everyone's side of the story and have made up my own version of events. I could never understand how someone could let their baby go. It does bother me that I have another brother out there somewhere though, and a nephew as well. Two other innocent people in all of this. I've found him on Facebook and check in every now and then, but we've never met or spoken. It was never my lie to fix, but it's still something I struggle with to this day. I love my dad for taking me on as one of his own – anyone can father a child but it takes a real man to be a dad – and I will always love him for that.

My life has taught me that everything is a lie and everything is a con. To begin with it was my family, then I came to realise my government was also doing the same. I've been saying throughout this book that money isn't real. It's only real because we think it is. It's all a con and it is all bullshit. Let me explain.

Our government hypnotises us and leads us to believe that we all have to become employees and work 40+ hours a week until we are nearly dead, the whole fucking thing is rigged. We are told we have to pay taxes on the money we earn, then again on the money we spend. We are told we should save money and spend money paying our debts off, i.e. our mortgages/ bank loans, etc. People do this without asking any questions because it's what we're taught to do. We're taught to leave school, get a job, get a house, get married and have kids – then spend the rest of our lives paying for all of it. In doing this the person stays poor, forever. The poor person then keeps themselves poor by buying goods which are no good whatsoever in the long term. They piss money down the drain buying designer clothes, designer bags, cars, motorbikes, flat screen TVs in every room, expensive furniture and a fridge that could be used as a spare room.

The rich person buys assets; they invest in gold. Your goal shouldn't be to move up the ladder in your poorly paid job where they have you over a barrel. Your goal should be to beat the system. A poor person will spend their savings on a new car, or they will get it on finance and piss the money down the drain every month, then trade it in every few years for eternity. They'll be doing this from their income working that dead end job where they look forward to their measly pay rise every year – which actually turns out to be a pay cut due to inflation.

A rich person will do something different, they will buy an asset, then use that asset to buy the car. If they buy an asset then makes money off that asset then they don't have to use any of their money at all.

For example, there are two people, person A and person B.

Person A was born poor with a poor man's mind. Person B was born poor but has an entrepreneur's mind. Both get £150,000 in inheritance. Person A thinks he's rich and decides he wants a new house and a new car (this is without a holiday, new clothes and a flash watch). The modest car is £30,000 and the modest house is £200,000. He buys the car for 30k, leaving him to put a down payment of £120,000 on the house; he then spends the best years of his life paying off the remaining 80,000 that he owes whilst running the car into the ground. He remains poor for the rest of his life.

Person B, the entrepreneur, uses his £150,000 inheritance and goes straight out and spends the whole lot on one asset, a shabby but solid house which needs some paint and some cosmetic work doing to it. He cleans it up, paints it and makes it presentable. The entrepreneur then rents that house out for a steady income each month. Meanwhile, as his income starts to pour in, he visits the bank. He borrows £180,000 on the strength of his new asset (the house he just bought which has now been valued at £180,000 after a spruce up and a lick of paint). Now, with the money he has borrowed he buys another house for £150,000 and rents that out to another family, leaving him £30,000 to invest, and so on. Before long he has lots of steady income, the tenants are paying the bank for him, he doesn't have to work and he has a brand-new car on finance – which his tenants are also paying. That's the fundamental difference between someone who knows the system is a con and someone who doesn't and believes the bullshit. You don't need 150k inheritance. All you need is a small deposit and to be able to think outside the box and understand that it is all a con.

Millionaires and billionaires stay rich because they can't be taxed on the shares that they hold within a company. Shares are still investments, but they fluctuate. Because of this fluctuation they are known an as unrealised gain. The millionaire/billionaire has the money but they don't have it – because they haven't sold it. Like an uncertain certainty. However, if they want to go to a bank and borrow vast amounts of money then they can use these stocks as collateral. So basically, they stay rich because they can buy something based on what they have but the government cannot tax them on it because theoretically they don't have it. Which is what the millionaires and billionaires do, have done, and will continue to do until the end of time to stay rich; and at the other end of the spectrum is why the poor people stay poor. You just have to be the one who's using the con and make it work for you.

Everyone around me who I have ever trusted, my family, my government, my doctors and many others. They're all liars. It's all one big fat lie, a scam, a fraud, a con. I figured out the bullshit a long time ago. And when I did, I decided it was me who was going to be in charge of the cons for a change.

My parents will read this one day. I hope they won't be disheartened about some of the things I've written about but I've had to get it out as part of the journey. There are other things I wanted to say but didn't, as I feel some things are best left unsaid, but the parts that I felt crucial to the map have been included. Lots of it I will never understand. They once sent me to bed because I did an Oliver Twist and complained that I was hungry. My father told me that he and my mother would go without food so I could eat. They then ordered a Chinese takeaway. For them.

There were so many signs and issues when I think about it that weren't ever looked into; the agonizing stomach cramps, the worms in my stools, pulling my hair out until the neighbour noticed the bald patches, holding my breath until I passed out, and wetting the bed. I have brought these things up a few times over the years. Each time I was met with the cop out of amnesia, so no responsibility can be taken for any actions – because that way they never really happened.

Getting sober and giving up drugs has been the hardest thing I've ever had to do, and I've never felt so alone in this world since losing my grandparents. They were the two people always closest to me even though they were the ones that lived the furthest away. Whilst in recovery I feel like I've had to suffer in silence and go it alone for pretty much the whole stretch of the last two and a half years. When I moved house and split with my ex, I was at my lowest point and nobody came to help when I was both physically and mentally broken to pieces. I've come to the realisation that I really am alone in this world. I just wish my grandparents were here and could see me sober.

For many people, families can be toxic, especially in broken homes. I liken it to keeping snakes as pets, it's absolutely fine as long as you keep them at a safe distance.

I have to say, though, that Christmases in our house were happy. This was the one time of year that everyone was guaranteed to be smiling, and there was plenty of food, and presents. My father worked his arse off to provide for us and gave me a warm bed, food and a place to live. I may have only had slimy pickle sandwiches, but my mother still made them for me.

I do have some good memories from being a kid, but there is a major difference between my mother and father regarding the ones that aren't so good. And that is my father has said he is sorry. My mother has never apologised, for anything, ever. I think this is why my mind won't leave the past alone. I will never forget a certain person saying that I am looking for the apology that I'm never going to get, and that is a tough pill to swallow; like the snake when it doesn't apologize for biting you. Why would it? It's a snake. That same person told me that we grow into the person that we needed as a child. Heavy shit.

CHAPTER 14

Devil Wears Cartier

The Cartier Con

This con is the one I was telling you about that I regretted and never did again. It would have been incidental if it wasn't for that reason, but I've included it as it is the only con that I ever felt shame for. It is one that could've netted me a lot of money like some of the others, and if it wasn't for a certain moral compass holding me back then I would have. Pulling a con on a hundred people for £10 will net you the same amount as pulling it on one person for £1,000. Some people would argue it is the same, but it isn't. And I just couldn't do the latter. Companies, yes; individuals, absolutely not. I did one con that netted me a lot more than that. And I'm not proud of it.

I'd been kicking around a few ideas of what to do next. I'd been making a lot of money but I'd been spending it too. Do you remember me telling you about my early memories of being up in the front seat with my dad in his '61 Mk2 Ford Zephyr? Well, this had started something in me as I've loved classic cars ever since.

My first ever real classic car was a Mk1 Ford Cortina GT with the propeller blade taillights. It had a 1500cc engine and was rear wheel drive; my uncle had got it for me and we spent the summer fixing it up. After that it was a Mk2 Ford Consul, it was the same body shape as my dad's old car except it was the cheaper model (Ford made what they called the three graces – the Ford Consul, Zephyr and Zodiac). The Consul was the cheapest, then the Zephyr and finally the Zodiac, with the engine size and trim package changing as the models progressed. My Consul wasn't shiny like my dad's, instead it was painted in red oxide, to cover the filler and the shoddy weld repairs that had been done to it.

The car was shocking when I think back. I remember my dad taking me a long way to go and pick it up, he told me it was a piece of shit, which it was – but I wouldn't listen. I'd already fallen in love with it the second we pulled around the corner. I paid the full asking price and we left.

It was exactly like the film Christine where Arnie Cunningham buys the '58 Plymouth Fury after his friend begs him not to. My new purchase, however, did not fix itself as the one did in the film, so unfortunately some good old fashioned hard work was required because 'you can't polish a turd'.

This was the kind of thing I spent my money on.

Within ten years I had purchased three Mk2 Consuls (one with a v8), a Vauxhall Magnum (v8), a Vauxhall Viva (v8), an AMC Javelin (big block v8), a Mk1 Escort and finally my big purchase – a 1970 Chevy Chevelle 454 big block v8. That thing was awesome. I called it grandma's grocery getter because it was big and green but it had huge rear tyres on and was as mean as you like. It sounded like thunder and was happiest when the pedal was put to the floor.

Other than that, I've owned motorbikes, sports bikes and dirt-bikes, a whole car park's worth of standard road cars and a few vans. I've lost count of the many, many thousands that I have spent on things with an engine that goes fast. I dread to think – but it was fun.

In the past I have had boxes and boxes full of gold, some pieces I paid vast amounts for from the likes of Trax NYC – diamond encrusted pharaoh heads and chains to go with them, fuck me I spent so much on that shit. I too fell for it the same way others do. Then there were the guns but we'll get into those later. And watches, but we've been through that and will do again.

I never really cared for designer clothing since I was really young, impressionable and easily led. Oh yes, and drugs and alcohol. I think I could've given Charlie Sheen and Keith Richards a run for their money when it came to the amount I have spent in my lifetime on that shit. Some of the parties were good but in the end the lows always outweigh the highs. A lot of it was given away as well, sometimes to those who needed it and sometimes to those who took advantage.

I'm not proud of my spending – it was for sale and I wanted it, or 'needed' it at the time. I am not a rich man; I had moments where I was doing okay – but it always went back to having nothing. Money comes and it goes – it isn't real, but that doesn't stop you feeling the pinch when it isn't there.

I think the reason I used to be so bad with money is because I never had any of it when I was young, I never had the chance to be able to learn how to manage it. My sister is the same – it comes in and it is spent, sometimes on ridiculous things that you have no need for, but it looks cool – so you want it. Take my money now.

I was going through a skint stage but it never took me long to get some coming in. I'd been looking online at Cartier watches and saw how much people were charging for them. Then I started looking through their jewellery range which is when I stumbled across the Cartier love bangle. They wanted between £3,500 and £5,000 for one of these, and it didn't even have an engine… I looked a bit closer and all it was, was a bangle, and it said Cartier on the inside, a hallmark and a number. It came with a piece of paperwork and it was in a nice box. A piece of white gold with a name on for £5,000, and people were paying it. What someone will pay for a piece of metal is shocking. I've been guilty of it, on many occasions. I've been tricked by the bullshit and the allure of the shiny metal, lots of us have for thousands of years. Where was I going to get one from? Or at least one that looks like it was made by Cartier?

I thought about my friend the jeweller. He had the ability to get one made up but he wasn't into anything that could come back on him. He had no qualms in selling some rocks on a metal band and charging the earth for it, but he wouldn't go putting names on his own work. What if I just got him to make the band? Then got the name put on it somewhere else? I didn't need to.

By now fake watches had made a big impression online. Companies were popping up left, right and centre and some of them were okay. The fakes were getting good and people were buying them, and I understand why. Why spend £10,000 when you can spend £250 and nobody really knows the difference? If you've got everything else in order then they won't. You'd still get the looks, people still think you have the money, and if you get robbed, you're only losing a couple of hundred pounds. What's the difference? Except you have a saving of £9,750…

Aside from the watches one company had started faking bracelets and bangles as well. They're everywhere now but they weren't then and the methods of detecting the fakes were nowhere near as good as they are now. I found the Cartier love bangle, and it looked great in the pics. I took a gamble and ordered one and it came through. What turned up in the post was even better than what was in the pics, it was well made and the finish on it was great. It looked like a real quality piece even under the loop, it had a full hallmark and the number 19 on it for the size. The box it came with was exceptional and the paperwork looked legit. I looked online for some genuine ones and went through everything. Everything they had, mine had, and you couldn't tell the two apart. I listed it online and allowed offers on it and before long they started to come in. I received a message from a buyer offering to pay £2,000. It was your typical lowball offer and I messaged back to say I would take £3,000. They came back and said they wanted it but wasn't willing to pay any more than £2,500 because there needed to be some wiggle room in it for them to make some profit. I explained that if I sold it to them then I'd be losing money because of eBay's percentage that they would be taking for their cut. With this they offered to deal outside of eBay and pay £2,500 straight into a bank account. I agreed, they paid – and I sent the bangle.

This had all been done over the course of an evening after a few beers and some Valium. When I woke the next day, the deal was done and it was too late to go back. Fuck it, they might never know.

It was months later that I got the message back. On the off-chance, they had taken it to a Cartier convention to get it looked at. It was found out to be fake by one of their specialists. A copy, but a good one, with thick gold plate – but it wasn't genuine. They wanted to know what I was going to do about it. I shut up shop, deleted the account and closed it down indefinitely. That was the last I heard from the buyer. There was nothing they could do about it because they were the ones that offered to deal outside of eBay, and in doing so they were not covered by eBay's money back guarantee. The gold, jewellery and watches in those days didn't have to go through an authentication centre so there was no third party to make the judgement on any discrepancies between the buyer and seller. The buyers can no longer say that the sellers have ripped them off and the sellers can't say that the buyer has sent anything Mickey Mouse back. Other people were at it too. And it's thanks to those scoundrels and the one-time me doing it that you have to thank for those security measures. That was the one time I have ever really ripped someone off and I felt fucking terrible for it. The reason I felt terrible for it was because I didn't know who the person was that was on the other end of it. I very much doubt it was a struggling family, bought by a husband to give to his sick wife, because they said they wanted to sell it on. But who knows. That was the one-time shitty thing I ever really did and I won't be doing it again.

CHAPTER 15

The Mourning Post

The Postal Service Con

This con was going to be easy – and enjoyable. I would be ripping off eBay, Parcelforce, UPS, the Royal Mail and FedEx. I was getting sick and tired of things with all of them and it was time to get my own back. I'd bought and sold thousands of items and they were coming from and going to many different places all over the world. I'd had issues with every postal service under the sun and eBay had taken a fortune from me in fees. The multi-national billion-pound organisation was charging far too much and they were getting greedy. They knew what I'd done with the bangle and couldn't prove it, but it didn't stop them billing me a stupid amount of money. Yes, I had done wrong, but they had taken far too many liberties and I wanted my money back.

Ever since I was a young lad, since my biscuit tin days, I had been trading watches in one way or another. As I grew, my watch obsession grew at the same time. I never really hung on to them very long because I'd love them immensely for a short while then the novelty would quickly wear off and I'd sell them on.

Because of my watch obsession and my love for a bargain, I would always have a load of different watches on my watch list online from all over the world. I got to know what prices they were going for, what was a bargain and when to walk away. You could get some right good bargains if you were willing to stay up until stupid hours of the morning. It was a hobby for me, aside from the money and kept me out of dumpsters.

I would find a watch, scrutinize it thoroughly from the pictures and contact the buyer. If the watch passed all the checks, then I would chuck in a cheeky offer and get the ball rolling. More often than not a seller would have a set price in their mind that they wanted, but occasionally you'd get a bite and they would be willing to end early for a quick, no hassle deal – as long as the funds were paid that evening.

I ordered one particular watch; a Breitling Colt – what is known among the Breitling community as a beginner's watch. Anyway, it was delivered to my doorstep. The trouble was – I wasn't home. This pissed me off profusely because by this point, I'd already had countless arguments with the postal services and workers about leaving stuff outside my front door. We didn't exactly live in Knightsbridge or Mayfair, and any junkie with a habit to feed could've picked it up while on his jollies. It was then and there that I decided the neighbourhood was going to start having a series of robberies – only the thief was going to be me.

I went back to the watches on my list for all the 'must haves' and started ordering. The idea was to go fishing –

throw out some offers and once hooked, start reeling them in, buy, buy, buy. The first thing you have to do is wait a week and not say a thing. Then the second port of call is to contact the seller to ask when they would be posting the watch (you already know they have because it usually tells you anyway but you're playing dumb). They tell you they have already posted it and to hang on a few more days because the post might be slow. You wait, patiently, then go back again to say it still hasn't arrived. The seller gets in touch with the postal service and finds out that they have already made a delivery. You know you haven't had a delivery because it arrived when you were out and you haven't signed for it – which you paid extra for in the first place, hence the reason it is called 'signed for' delivery. This is when you start to kick up a fuss. You have to picture in your mind what it would actually feel like to have just paid £2,500 for a watch that hasn't turned up. You'd be furious. You would be worried you weren't getting the money back – and you would act accordingly.

It's times like this I feel I would have been good at drama school because my method acting skills are second to none when there's two and a half grand on the line. I'd go apeshit and file a complaint with the postal service, the seller would from their end too. You'd keep the relationship between you and the seller as sweet as can be because, after all, it was neither of your faults and you're both victims in this situation. You both want either your money or your goods back so now you've joined forces against the one common enemy – the postal service. They were at fault for the services they haven't provided.

It was their duty to get said parcel signed for – which is their fault and something they are bang to rights for.

One of the postal workers came round to my house, he wanted me to sign some paperwork to say that I hadn't received the watch, have a quick chat, then he would go back to his depot to file a report. Within a few weeks you get a refund and the seller gets to keep his money too. Everyone's a winner, except the postal service, but fuck 'em – they owe me. It worked like a dream so that was what I did every time I ordered a watch and it didn't arrive. If I was home and the doorbell went, then I wouldn't answer the door – hoping it would be left on the doorstep. I always made sure I requested 'signed for' delivery and I never allowed any parcels to be put in a 'safe place'. It didn't work every time, but at the beginning, one in three would be waiting for me – and the ones that did get to me were moved on, but for the one in three – chit ching, another free watch.

I had to be careful because I had to move the watches on after I had taken possession of them, as one has to be with essentially stolen watches. It would be a bit iffy had I sold the very same watch on the same site that I bought it from, but I did. I'd wait a while, in order for the dust to settle then re-sell the same watch but on a different account. I had a whole box of straps, some rubber and some leather, 20,21 and 22mm – in order so they could be swapped, even if only for photo's sake and I wouldn't include the box, guarantee card or paperwork in the pictures. If a potentially interested buyer asked about the paperwork, then I would message them privately with the requested photo proof that I did, in fact, have the box and paperwork. The operation went, well, like clockwork. I had to be a bit careful about pulling the same con more than once with the same company. The absolute godsend for me was that Covid had hit by this point and the world had gone mad. A lot of people were still at home bored, listing and buying watches like crazy but the workforce was back out on the street. I had taken full advantage of the fact that we were in a worldwide pandemic, and there was no better time than that to get the cons in full swing.

Lots of people got rich during the pandemic. I have spoken to drug dealers that have said it was the best time to be in business and that they'd welcome another one anytime. People go all out when they are stuck at home, bored and have money to spend. And there is money out there. I don't care what anyone says, recession, inflation, or the cost of toilet roll going up – a lot of people have or can find money to spend when they really want something.

The watches that I, unfortunately, had to spend money on I made sure I got them for a good price to begin with, so that was just a case of wrapping them back up, creating a better ad than the seller I bought from and move it on. I either made a small profit or broke even after fees. I've always been good at selling – there just isn't a big enough buzz in it for me.

So that is the top and bottom of it really. I conned her majesty's Royal Mail, Parcelforce, UPS and FedEx and I enjoyed every minute of it. It ended because I took it too far. I knew I was supposed to keep the number of times I scammed each company to a minimum, but I went against my own advice and pulled it on UPS once too often. I tried it again and it didn't work. It was around five years ago now and they had already started hotting up with these types of cons. I had one of the UPS workforce come to my house as well. He basically told me he knew I had taken the watch and that I was trying to pull a fast one. I was outraged by this. I had done my usual performing arts routine imagining the audacity of this man saying this to me when I had just lost £5,500. It didn't work. He knew it, I knew it, but I stuck to my guns. I took matters further and filed a complaint, only for the matter to be dropped in UPS' favour. This scam was over. It netted good money for such a short space of time and wasn't a bad day at the office for a few clicks of a button. No-one was hurt, everybody gained – except the postal service. And I hate those fuckers.

It was around this time that I was splitting up with my wife for the final time. We'd split up before and got back together but now it really wasn't working. She was and still is my best friend in the whole wide world apart from my brother and my friend Karl, and if I was splitting up from anyone then I didn't want it to be her. I'd caused her too much heartache over the years. She knew all my inner demons and all the skeletons in my closet had been unloaded onto her. It was too much for one person to take and for some reason we often brought out the worst in each other.

When we first met, we were inseparable and spent every possible moment together, awake and asleep.

I think in those first few years we must have had the equivalent of a thirty-year marriage. I miss her dearly but it's difficult when your head says one thing and your heart says another. I still think we could give it another shot but we have definitely got on better since we got our own place each. It's so hard when you love someone but all you seem to do is destroy each other. It's a hard thing to accept that you're never going to be able to make it right, as much as you both want to. You'd think that love conquers all but sometimes that just isn't the case. It isn't fair because I want her to be happy, but more than that I want us to be happy together.

We have a great son and if nothing else we seem to have dragged him up okay. We all still hang out together and are a good little family unit. You never know, maybe one day it will work itself out. She told me she doesn't want to see too much of me because she's worried that she will fall in love with me again. I've never really fallen out of love with her but I think it's different for guys than it is for women. What do I know? I've fallen in love three times and I don't have any room for another. If it doesn't work, I know I will spend the rest of my days alone. I won't be alone because there will be people around me, but I will definitely be by myself. I must admit, being able to watch documentaries on bank robberies, heists and organized crime instead of Big Brother and Love Island does have its perks.

So, from now on I would be single, free to do as I pleased with no-one asking me what I was up to. Shit was about to get real as the stakes would be upped, tenfold.

CHAPTER 16

Trick Or Treat

The Diamond Con

By now I was stone cold sober, and single – and I was feeling the pain in more ways than one. My addictions were a big reason for the break up and it had taken its toll on both of us. Being sober helped in some ways and made things harder in others. It was the only thing that would help to ease my racing thoughts and slow my mind. I was OCD before, but now I'm OCD with a super charger and infinite fuel. The good thing about an addiction is you're only left with one worry. It's a fucking big worry but there is only one of them, which is finding whatever it is that you're addicted to – everything else comes second, and when you're stoned the other worries don't seem that much of a problem anymore. A bill needs paying – find more product; the missus is sick of you – find more product; someone dies – find more product. It's a never-ending cycle.

When you're sober you have everything to worry about – not only that it has now been magnified. Sobriety isn't for the weak.

Since being sober my wife and others around me have started telling me I have ADHD because of all the hyper focusing on things which has become more apparent since giving up the drink and drugs; they clouded my emotions but was my medicine. I had been clearly self-medicating for years in the only way I knew how. All I knew is that if I took enough of something then it would make me feel better, but if I took too much of it then it would make me feel worse. I was going to hit the next cons like a freight train at full speed and if I crashed then I only had me to worry about. Full steam ahead.

I approached the next con the same way they used to do it back in the swinging '60s in London, England. The likes of Freddie Foreman (originally from South of the river but moved to the East-End) and Charlie Kray (the East End) used to take part in a scam known as the long-firm fraud. Basically, you would set up a company somewhere and call it what you like – let's call it 'Eddie's Electricals, for argument's sake. Eddie's Electricals would specialize in electrical goods that were starting to become popular after WW2 – washing machines, tumble driers, cookers, fridges, freezers, heaters, vacuum cleaners, etc. The company would order in goods from a supplier and sell them on. After a level of trust had been established between the supplier and Eddie's Electricals, items could be bought on credit or 'sale or return', meaning that large quantities of these items could be taken to sell on with the money coming later on, or the money coming once the items had been sold. Of course, the money for the items never came. As soon as the company had taken possession of the big shipment of goods, they would shut up shop and vanish – then sell the goods on at a third of the price and start the whole process again. Magic – everyone's a winner. I was going to do this, but with diamonds.

I set up many different accounts using different bank accounts and got the ball rolling. I was buying and selling on the side anyway so it didn't take long to build up some positive feedback with sales under my belt.

At first, I would buy small stones; you can get some right bargains if you know where to look and are happy to have a diamond under the magic 1.00ct, and they are always easy to move – whether they're loose or set into a ring. The best places I have found are in America and China; they have good diamonds to offer and are dealing in the millions so it's not as if they'd miss one or two going astray. Avoid India like the plague. I tried that and the country seemed to be jam-packed with scallywags and scoundrels that would probably rip their own mothers off – great if you're looking for a box of glass or a pile of dog shit. One guy sold me some emeralds – 'Rare Columbian Emeralds' apparently – they fucking weren't, they were made from actual glass. I got my money back, sheister. It turned out I had bought a load from him, all in separate purchases. I would have ruined his business account in one fell swoop had he gone through with it. He'd spent a long time building it up and it would be a shame if one guy destroyed it all. He didn't – he paid up. Cheeky monkey.

China is cheaper but America has better quality – you get what you pay for. When it was time to strike a little while down the line, I would message the dealer first and say I had an order come in that needed 'x' number of diamonds, but they had to be perfect. I only wanted stones that were 1.00 carat or over in size and they had to be beautifully cut and polished. I would accept stones as low down as a 'J' colour but absolutely no less than that and even that was pushing it. I wanted VS clarity and upwards, which meant they could only have the very minutest of inclusions that could only be seen under magnification and flawless to the naked eye. And if possible, I wanted them to match. I wasn't too picky but I preferred round brilliant cuts or oval brilliant cuts because I was looking for the optimal dispersion of light – and they offered the best refraction, which is why an engagement ring glistens as the light bounces up into the person's eye as he or she is drooling over it. I would offer to buy as many as they had that fell within these guidelines as long as I got a cut-down price, which didn't really matter other than the lower the value then the less I would be paying in possible customs charges (which isn't like it is now). I would spout the same shit to all of them and they all fell for it. I put them to work then stood back and waited while they scurried around looking for anything that matched my description because it was going to be in their interest, or so they thought. Sometimes they would have loads kicking around, all matching and all perfect, and other times there would only be a few.

I had cash waiting to spend because I was doing okay with the scrap gold at the time. I was only paying between £8-£10 per gram and the daily rate was about £15. It's surprising what people have lying around at home when they're a bit strapped for cash. They think because it's broken then it isn't worth much, but gold is gold. It was more than they would get from a jeweller.

That being said, the stones were costing a lot of money initially and there was going to be a short while for the turnaround, so I could only deal with a few diamond dealers at a time. It was okay because I'd have them all on rotation so while one was in the process of sending, another was on the lookout to see what they had in stock. Everybody was up for it and everybody had something – every, single, time. I had diamonds coming in from all over the place. I already had an idea of a way to get rid of them but I'd be keeping them for now.

The idea was simple: get the stones, swap the stones, then send the Mickey Mouse ones back. I'd pulled this con before and it worked. I'd ordered a yellow oval diamond; it measured just over 7.5mm x 5.5mm (this can vary depending on the cut and depth of the stone as we've already been through). Anyway, I hated the stone, it was the spitting image of some canary yellow cubic zirconia's I had bought in to put inside a Fabergé style egg for decoration. It was of Tutankhamun – one my grandad made for me. I compared the diamond with a couple of the CZs and they were almost identical. So, I thought, fuck it. I cut open the sealed container which housed the diamond and swapped it, re-sealed it back up with superglue and sent it back – and never heard a thing.

Lightbulb moment.

I varied what I said to each party after the goods had arrived. To some I said the diamonds weren't to my liking and to others I told them they weren't genuine. Either way I was sending them back. The sellers that only sold sealed packages to me never cottoned on. They got lost in the spaghetti junctions of the diamond skullduggery business of buying and selling. By the time they had switched hands a few times it was difficult to tell who had, for sure, lifted the stones. Was it me? Was it the postal worker in the UK? Customs? A US or Chinese postal worker? Someone in their building?

More often than not they came back and told me not to buy from them again. The parcel had shown up as delivered so my refund came through and there wasn't a lot they could do about it. There was nothing they could prove or disprove. Hence the reason why they brought in third parties, so there can be no discrepancy – you have me to thank for that, and you're welcome.

The good thing with this con is you don't have to pull it that many times before you strike gold – or diamonds. For argument's sake, let's call it a grand per stone – it doesn't take long for it to start piling up. The companies that sold me fairly large quantities were pissed. Occasionally I'd send back some Mickey Mouse stones and some genuine ones back at the same time, just to throw a spanner in the works. Why would someone send back a genuine diamond? Then more questions would be asked. Maybe he is telling the truth. You never know, they could have opened one package and just tested one rock. It worked well and eventually I had run out of dealers to buy from. Luckily for me you could have as many accounts as you wanted then, but I couldn't pull the same con twice on the same diamond dealer. Ebay didn't really care either, and as long as they got their cut, they were happy.

There is something hugely satisfying about an envelope of diamonds. They are very pretty, but not only that, you know there are lots of things you could get in exchange for them.

I remember having a conversation with my boss/ partner at the jewellery shop/ I asked him what he thought about the introduction of HPHT and CVD diamonds and whether he thought they would affect the diamond trade at all. He said they'd be a fart in the wind and would be a big deal at first then fizzle out the same way cubic zirconia's did back in the day. I'm too young to remember that but I told him I thought he was wrong. I thought they'd likely push the 'ethical' side to owning lab created stones to the younger, 'woke' generation.

I don't think earth-mined diamonds will be phased out completely, but since 2022 when earth-mined stones were at a peak, their value had dropped by 34% in 2024 and will likely keep dropping. The lab-grown gems have become substantially more affordable, and while they may cost significantly less and are a sustainable alternative to earth-mined diamonds, this means they are less rare. And what does that mean? Yes – their re-sale value is going to be worth fuck all.

I had pulled it off which left me with a safe full of envelopes containing lots of precious stones that I had to get rid of. If only there was another con that I could use them for – I could do with some breakfast, at Tiffany's…

CHAPTER 17

Greatest Guns

The Weapons Con

It was a cold winter's night and I'd just put the fire on. I hadn't long moved into a new detached house, about nine months before. It was a nice street where the neighbours actually spoke to one another, the kind of street where if you were a week behind on cutting your lawn then the busy-bodies would be pulling faces and then the comments would start, polite, but they couldn't help themselves. One has to keep up one's appearances, doesn't one.

All the street lights worked and even the binmen and postmen said, 'Good Morning'. There wasn't any rubbish in the roads and everybody's cars were smart, with all the original wheels on, and not one dent between them. Nobody had late night parties or barbecues and there wasn't a trampoline in sight. Even the dogs were of a higher class, they didn't bark or try and maul the paperboy, no Staffies, Pit Bulls or Bulldogs here – and everyone was safely inside by 9pm.

I was settling down to watch some cop programme on TV when I heard a noise coming from the front of my house. The good thing about where I now live is the acoustics. You can hear a pin drop by the way the houses are built – all nestled into a neat little cul-de-sac. No-one ever came to my house – not at night. I quickly looked out of the window but all I could see was a small torch pointing back at me. What the fuck is that? I opened the door then instantly realised that the shit had finally caught up with me and it was about to hit the fan. It was a team of Exeter's finest, from the specialist firearms unit – all armed and dressed in black tactical gear. They had baseball caps on and bulletproof vests. These weren't your local bobbies on the beat.

Let's go back a bit, a few months or so.

I was free and single and allowed to get up to all sorts of capers – anything that my idle hands could think of. Since I was a young boy, I have been interested in weapons. It started with lock knives, flick knives and butterfly knives. My friend Karl and I used to make bows and arrows and shoot marbles and ball bearings from a catapult/slingshot over at the factory across the road causing untold costly damages.

When we were 12, we joined the army cadet force and as soon as we turned 13, they let us have a uniform and handle our first rifles, which were the L98A1 cadet GP (general purpose) rifles. They were single shot machines capable of firing a 5.56 x 45mm round effectively up to around 500 metres. They were based on the British Army's SA80 fully automatic/semi-automatic selective firing models. They were really only training rifles but I fell in love with mine as soon as I held it. I'd only had air rifles before, my uncle bought me my first break barrel air gun and a tin of .22 pellets. I used to shoot it with my dad in our back garden.

Every few years we were lucky enough to go to Spain, my grandparents lived there and would pay for our tickets to go out and see them. It was the highlights of the year other than Christmas and one of the best bits about it was my brother and I could go to the markets and buy whichever lethal looking blade we took a fancy to and could bring it back to England, without a care in the world when it came to security. This was way before 9/11 and you could pretty much bring back whatever you liked. My grandad brought a sword back once and so did I. Mine was in a suitcase – his was inside an old telescope. As I got older my collection grew. I went to London once and brought back a bayonet from WW2, and a rocket launcher. The bayonet I took to school which I very nearly got expelled for because Karl took it out and started throwing it around the class – as you do; the rocket launcher I sold to a college buddy called Plesner in the toilets at college.

When I got to university it was the first time that I had money to waste, so along with the purchase or two of drugs, gold and precious stones I decided to buy some firearms.

Handguns were all very much illegal since the school shootout at Dunblane a few years previous, but you could still purchase semi-automatic blank firers and revolvers. We've spoken about the 9mm blank firer that I bought from the pawn broker that I did my Rolex switch in – the real steel ex-forces weapon that had been converted to fire blanks only. Well, in those days these could be easily converted back to firing live rounds. All you needed was a drill, some drill bits, a file, some odds and sods and the know-how and you were good to go – until the powers that be decided to end all the fun.

While I was there, I bought a Brocock ME .38 revolver, which was perfectly legal at the time. The reason it was legal was because it only fired pellets, originally. This worked because you had a cartridge, shaped just like a bullet, which was a gas cylinder that you had to manually pump up. You stuck the pellet in the end, and bang. It was only supposed to be pumped up to a maximum of eight times so as not to damage the seals. My brother and I could get 20 pumps into them, 21/22 at a push. And that thing fired, fuck me was it powerful. Then the police realised that the underworld had figured out how to kill people with them. There were two ways of going about this. The first option was to place a .22 calibre round into a brass sleeve and put it straight into the cylinder. You had to bend the firing pin or better still, weld another to the hammer because the round was made for rim-fire only, meaning that the firing pin had to strike the edge and not the centre of the round. Once you had done these simple steps you had a live-firing weapon. It was only a .22 calibre round which our American cousins over the pond would deem as pitiful, but to most of us Brits is pretty cool. If you wanted something more powerful, that didn't just go bang, make you feel like a gangster and help you get rid of a rabbit or three then you'd need to go for option two – drilling or milling out the barrel. This way you can put a .38 calibre round straight into the cylinder and before you know it, pop goes the weasel and Billy Big Guns can come out to play. This way should give you around 200 shots before cracking the frame and blowing your hand off.

I wasn't much into my twenties when I met my ex-wife, she had a young boy and she didn't want there to be a vast number of guns around him. I agreed it probably wasn't such a good idea and stored everything I owned at the in-laws' garage. Years went by and I forgot about them. So much so that my mother in-law decided it was her civil duty to hand them into the police. Shock horror. My life's collection since I was a boy surrendered to the boys in blue (a shame because there were some real nice pieces in there). Hey ho.

Fast forward 15 years or so later and we are separating. Me, in my infinite wisdom, decides to take up collecting again. Now I have some real money that I could do some real damage with, the only trouble is, is that every fucking handgun, or anything that even resembles a handgun has been banned or at least is hard to get hold of. By now the only thing that you can buy is a blank handgun made from pot metal with extremely weak blanks, a CO_2 gas-powered pellet handgun that fires pellets (I say fires, I mean you can pull the trigger and watch the pellet fall out the end), or a replica, made from die-cast metal that cannot, and will not fire anything. Boy has the world changed, and fast.

As always, when I get an idea in my head I will research it until my eyes bleed. If someone tells me I cannot do something and I want to do it, my brain will not let me stop until I can find a way around it. And if there's a way, and there's almost always a way, then I will find it – even if it isn't double legal. Basically, I wanted a handgun, either a 9mm semi-automatic, or a .38 calibre revolver. Now, with the change in the laws the penalty for owning just one could land you five years in prison, not including the penalty for firing one, having the bullets for one, or the possible penalty for how you got one in the first place – for ONE.

At the time of writing there are still a handful of ways of owning a handgun in England. These are: have a licence – nope, that's illegal, can't do it. Unless you're a squaddie, part of the police firearms unit or 007. Can't do it. Steal one – nope, unless you can get hold of a few surviving war veterans that haven't handed theirs in or a few top crims who are willing to do a five-year stretch and willing to let you break into their stash, forget it. Make one – you can build a pipe gun from a thick steel tube if you have access to shotgun shells – nope, it technically isn't a hand gun, it's big, inaccurate and will probably blow your face off.

There have been some impressive pieces made in people's workshops and in prisons, because something as simple as a staple gun can be used. Essentially all you need is a barrel, chamber, hammer, trigger and projectile and bob's your uncle. But unless you want to be a laughing stock instead of gangster no1 with your piece of steel pipe and elastic bands wound together, then nope – try again. Print one – 3-D printers at the time of writing are in their infancy, especially in the UK, and with spy technology on the up, the bastards are going to know when you start ordering metal moving parts on the internet and are going to get suspicious if you have been ordering from the dark web – nope, fuck that. Convert one. Hmmm, but what are you going to convert? The blank guns these days are shit and anything else just wouldn't work. Or would it? It was worth a try.

To start with I ordered a bunch of blank semi-automatic handguns. These were legal, they looked good and they were handy for scaring birds, but that was about it. I went into my workshop and reverse engineered each one. I'd ordered a few of the same models because I knew there were going to be hiccups along the way, and I wasn't one for waiting around for the next delivery. I knew once I'd started it, it was going to be a manic race until I found the answer. The model I chose to start with, was the Walther PPK. Different sites had slightly different versions so I ordered a few from each site – some had the magazine release catch on the bottom, and some were on the side. Some were bright orange, and some were blue and silver; other than that, they were pretty much the same.

The good thing about the PPK is it's easy to disassemble. If you pull the slide back as far as it can go while pulling the trigger guard down then you can lift it up and it slides right off, spring included. Straight away I decided to bin the orange models. They were cheap, poorly-made and useless. The silver and blue ones were better. They were made from zinc alloy but they were solid and if they could withstand a blank round then they could live-fire, but for how long and safely is another issue entirely. The magazines were fine. With the PPK, it only houses a few rounds but I could see that a 9mm live would fit – it was okay diameter-wise but a short would be needed – acquiring these would be the last thing. The barrel was weak, not hollow, and useless so it had to come off completely – grinder, cutting disc and file off – check. Now I needed a new barrel. I went online and ordered myself some lengths of steel pipe. They had to have an inner diameter of at least 9mm for the bullets to pass through, be heavy-duty enough to withstand the power of a 9mm cartridge blast and not be too thick for the frame and slide. The steel pipe was ordered, delivered, measured, cut and filed – check.

Next, the frame had to be drilled out so the barrel could be placed in and soldered or welded. Being that it was a zinc alloy meant this wasn't too difficult to do. The steel pipe was then placed where it needed to be and hammered through the hole, then soldered in place; it couldn't be welded because of the heat, and working with zinc and steel was a ball ache. Eventually, I got to the point where it held, it wasn't great but it had some strength to it, I tried to break it with only my hands and couldn't. It would work. The solder was then filed until the slide could move freely over it. I almost had the finished article – check.

By now I was on my second try. I had almost given up at one point during the first attempt because I had melted some of the parts with the blowtorch during the heating process – plus I'd lost a spring and fuck knows where that was. I'd also bent the frame in the vice, I was going to throw the whole lot in the bin and scrap the idea, thinking it was too difficult for a reason. Then I watched a documentary called ghost guns. Basically, about people producing their own weapons because they couldn't get hold of the real thing. In one part there was a bit with two guys in Malaysia or somewhere. They literally had a shed and some primitive tools and they were producing replica Colt 1911s and selling them on. This gave me newfound hope because if these fuckers could do it, then so could I. You live and learn, and practise makes perfect.

Now to put everything back together, make sure it works as it should, disassemble again, file a bit here and there, reassemble, disassemble, and put back together – check. I sanded the whole frame because originally it came in two colours. I then polished the bare metal. It now had a shiny alloy finish. I bought some gun oil and oiled the moving parts, and rubbed it over the bare metal before wrapping it in a cloth. First piece done. A 9mm Walther PPK semi-automatic. I hadn't fired it yet but everything hit where it was supposed to so there was no reason why it shouldn't. I was happy with the product and would give it a test run later.

I looked into maybe converting a pellet gun semi-auto, but it wouldn't work. It could probably be done but with the amount of work involved I may as well build a gun from scratch, like those two Malaysian guys in their shed. Fuck that – I was a fan of working smarter, not harder. The 9mm semi-auto box was ticked. Now I wanted a revolver.

The blank revolvers that could be bought in the UK were shit. They would blow apart as soon as any force was put within the cylinders. A zinc frame is one thing, but fuck, using a zinc rotating cylinder in a revolver – that's asking for trouble. I was going to have to source further afield. They had some good blank revolver models on the German market but there was no chance of getting them through British customs. They had some awesome looking snub-nosed .38s. They were licensed by Smith & Wesson and were extremely well-made, they had the Smith & Wesson badge embossed on them and came with the textured removable grips. I had to get 1, or 2, 3, 5, 10, more, more, more – just like the drugs. But how was I going to get them over the border?

My grandad died which left my nan alone in Spain. I went out to see her and be with her. I loved my grandparents more than anything in the whole world. They were my saviours and kept me from going under. I would go out to visit them every few years and they would always bring me back from the brink of whatever I was going through. It didn't matter how many times I fucked up – they were always there to pick up the pieces and offer some direction. I viewed my grandparents as if they were my second mum and dad. They had looked after me part-time since birth; to begin with they had me at the weekends and would take me out to places. I have fond memories of being tucked into bed and I knew their house was safe. The sheets had a different smell and they were crisp and clean. They had plenty of food and apple juice and they loved me.

It was my nan's plan to come back to England now that my grandad was gone. She was alone and wanted to be closer to family. This meant there was going to be a lorry that was coming all the way from Spain to England with my nan's stuff. There is no way customs would be opening up every box and checking each item. Now was my chance. I ordered the Smith & Wesson's and had them shipped straight to Spain from Germany. The postal service was still behind the times in Spain and if they were any more chilled out then they would be on a full-time siesta. The guns arrived. My nan didn't even have to sign for them. Most of them were just thrown over the iron gates and some were even given to next door. I ordered one the first time, then two, then three, and batches of three after that. My nan knew what they were – she asked and I told her. I didn't have to lie to her. I told her they were starter pistols which they essentially are, although there weren't many races that were going to be started with them. She used to work for the same guy as me remember? – the 357 Magnum, the BMW and the Range Rover up in the Hacienda on the hill? She used to also look after the villa while he was away. My nan knew the score and knew what I was up to. She knew I was a bit dodgy but nothing that bad in her eyes. I wasn't a 'wrongun' put it that way. I asked her to open one of the boxes up to check that everything was there. She said it was a beautiful gun, ha-ha, my nan, well into her seventies telling me how beautiful this piece was. She was class. I told her they were impossible to get in England and would sell for a fortune. They weren't top venting like the shit over in the UK, these were front venting – which meant the barrels weren't plugged and much less of a ball ache to convert. My nan put them into boxes stacked two high with the rest of her belongings on top. The guns were small being that they were only snubbies with short barrels. You could get 12 in a box easy and they hardly took up any room. The boxes were taped up, labelled 'front room', 'bedroom', 'kitchen' and 'garage'. If anything was to go down my nan already knew to say she knew nothing about them, that she'd never seen them before, and that it was nothing to do with me. She may have looked like a sweet old grandma but she knew how to play the game. How do you think my grandparents had two villas in Spain and property in England? My grandad retired at 40 and my nan never worked, well, she never did anything that the government knew about anyway. They realised the bullshit around the same age that I did and knew how to play it to their advantage.

The guns arrived in the lorry, fresh off the boat. I unloaded them and stored them away. We had pulled it off. Nan and grandson-1, customs and police-0. I wasn't going to stop there. I wanted more. I'd seen a YouTube video of people shooting firearms in what looked like some third world housing project somewhere. The guns they had were made by WinGun. Basically, they were .22 pellet gun revolvers that you had to use a CO_2 cylinder which was hidden in the grip. I'd decided against pellet guns originally. They definitely wouldn't work for the semi-autos, but for the revolvers, they were different. These could be easily converted to fire a .22 live round because they were made to fire .22 pellets! The pellets worked by inserting them into a brass or steel sleeve then placing that into the chamber, they slotted straight in. These brass shells were double handy because they provided extra strength to the cylinder, firing a .22 round from these would be safe as 'ouses. The barrel didn't need to be drilled out at all because the bullet was narrow enough to slide straight through. All you had to do to the gun was take off the hammer, fit a firing pin and a stronger spring and you were away. It wasn't exactly large calibre shooting but you could do some damage with it.

The next problem was, again, getting them home. This actually proved to be a piece of piss and nothing like the Germany - Spain - England shenanigans. I found out you could get certain items back to the UK providing you had a good reason for doing so. We had re-enactment groups which were basically men and women dressing up in WW1 and WW2 clothing and fantasizing about wartime Britain. In order to complete their outfit, they needed weapons, not live-firing but something they could use as replicas. If you were a member of one of these groups then you could buy the guns.

To start with I printed off a certificate with my own fake identification number, I then went online and ordered some WinGun .38s. They came through with no questions asked and they were good, solid and with a nice finish. Each one had a photocopy of the certificate I had scanned and sent to them attached to the parcels so

I know they were looked at in customs – so I did it again. The second time didn't go as well as the first, because the online site that I purchased from had contacted the re-enactment group to confirm who I was. They said they'd never heard of me. The club captain then emailed and asked me why I was creating fake certificates to say that I was a member of their group when I wasn't? I made some poor excuses, smoothed it over as best I could with some light-hearted bullshit then got the hell out of there. It was a close call.

I still wanted more guns because I was on a roll and wanted to keep the buzz going. I had a think, waited a while for the dust to settle then put in for membership to join the club. I would become a full member, receive their monthly magazine and be invited to their re-enactments at Saunton Sands and anywhere else. It was actually pretty cool; they would go as extras for war films all dressed up to the nines and ready for battle. They did one with Tom Hardy. I didn't go; it wasn't my thing but I could start to see why people did it. Each member was given a membership card in order to purchase their weapons, then they could buy what they wanted and legally own them, transport them and have them on one's person. All I had to do was pay a small monthly fee and I was in.

At first, I thought I wasn't going to be going to any of the outings, playing army and masturbating over times gone by whilst looking like a complete tool – I just wanted the card. It turned out I never did go along but I understood the attraction. Now I could order as many as I liked – legally. I stuck to two per site as I had to be a bit careful. It would look a tad obvious had I ordered 20 and I'd already had a close shave.

Eventually all the WinGun .38 arsenal was purchased and they were on their way; to add to the collection that were waiting to be converted. It still wasn't enough. I wanted more. And I had to move fast because the laws were rapidly getting worse. The next stop was my favourite subject – antiques – but this time it was antique guns. Whilst doing some online learning and researching loopholes I found out you could still get hold of antique firearms but only if the ammunition was obsolete. If they had stopped producing ammunition then people had nothing to load the cylinders with – and therefore they couldn't be fired.

Or perhaps, could they?

The good thing about antique firearms is they haven't been deactivated. All the parts are fully moving, nothing has been welded up, plugged or butchered and it makes it a damn site easier when you want to make some whizz, pop, bangs. I'd already tried deactivated revolvers. I ordered a snub-nosed .38 Smith & Wesson that was an ex-police revolver. It cost me £500 and looked the bollocks. The trouble was it was fucked and there was no chance. It had been taken apart and the internals had been mutilated, the moving parts for the most part were no longer moving and it had been welded back together. It wasn't a complete waste because the cylinder, grips and hammer could be used later on for something else. It was a shame that such a nice piece had been butchered so badly. Animals.

The only thing with the antiques was that they were rim-fire and pin-fire only. Centre-fire guns had been banned years ago because the crims had worked out that they could come in handy. The trouble with rim-fire is the only bullets available were the .22 calibre and these were far too small to fit the cylinders, plus, not very powerful. Also, the firing pin wouldn't hit where it was supposed to. The same with the pin-fire models. These were designed so the hammer would strike from the top of the gun. Back in the day the ammo had a spike protruding from the side of the shell casing, these needed to be struck in order to ignite the gun powder and push the bullet forward. Sleeves could be used on smaller rim-fire rounds to fit the chambers but again, there needed to be contact in the exact position. I needed to come up with the right ammunition and work on the hammers but that would have to wait.

I started ordering the guns in, small calibre .32s at first, then the .38s, then the big boys at .44. I was quite picky when choosing which guns I wanted. What I was buying was old but I didn't want anything that looked too old. Some of these things looked like they had come out of the ark and were more laughable than mean-looking. I wanted something I could load up and go, not have to start a coal fire to get the pistons going. The .32s arrived but they were tiny – much smaller than I had imagined. One was smaller than the old cap guns I used to play with as a kid. I imagined robbing a bank with it. Freeze, or I'll shoot – followed by laughter with the teller asking me if I'd been drinking. They looked like they would be used as the last line of defence, either in a lady's purse or in a guy's boot. They weren't going to be fit for purpose and unrealistic for the mass-market. The .38s were hard to get hold of and very few and far between. There were some for sale but you had to pay top whack for them and they only came around every so often, but when they did – I bought. The good thing about quite a lot of the .38s is they haven't really changed all that much in the last 150 years. They are pretty much the same style. I guess if it isn't broken then it doesn't need fixing – they found something that worked and stuck with it. The bulldogs were especially good, both American and British – they were expensive but worth it. There were Belgian copies of these as well, and they were good also. I ordered as many as I could.

The .44s and above were like hand cannons. They didn't really call them .44 calibre in those days, instead they were called 11mil (mm), etc. Some went up to 18mm. This was unnecessary (says the guy with the rocket launcher), some of these were 150 years old and I didn't want to be blowing a hole in the cylinders – or the moon. Antiques were the most expensive way to go around acquiring firearms and unless you have deep pockets then it probably isn't the best way to go. I had invested a fortune so I had to make it work. Again, I had pretty much sucked the market dry but my stores were full and it was time to get to work.

The first semi-auto I completed had taken me ages but I had learnt a few things along the way. I had so many guns I needed to convert but I didn't want to spend a year doing it so I adopted Henry Ford's idea. I built a small factory and a production line. There would be a disassembly area, a cutting area, a heat, metal, filing and sanding area, and an end of line assembly and quality control. By doing this I could speed things up a lot faster. It started off being fun but, like many other schemes, quickly turned into a full-time job. If I was to get busted during this phase then I would be well and truly fucked. 'Mr Cook has been charged with the possession, production and supply of illegal firearms in large quantities; how do you find him? Guilty as fuck your honour! Take him down….'. Not just yet.

The semi-autos were the quickest, cheapest and by far the easiest to do but the revolvers were expensive. I gave up with the .32s. They were small, fragile and quite frankly just looked shit. The .38s were great and so were the big boys, the .44s especially – they were my favourite. They were bulky but I liked that. They were solid and you could tell just by holding them that they weren't going to break. Some of these would last another 150 years, no problem – as long as the rozzers didn't get hold of them and ruin everybody's fun.

I still had the problem of no ammunition. I had already had an idea of how to do it; I hadn't just produced a load of guns and hoped for the best. I'd seen a few videos of idiots putting melted lead onto the tips of blanks and using them. I say idiots because some of them really were and it's no surprise why we have the shocking laws that we do in Britain. I've seen videos of blanks blowing up in people's faces as they were holding them without gloves or eye protection on. In one video a guy's gun mis-fired so he turned it around and stared directly down the barrel to see what the problem was. Excellent behaviour, and a sure way to discover whether Newton was correct with his findings on the laws of physics and motion. What they were doing was dangerous and asking for trouble.

If people want something they will go to great lengths in order to get it. And I was going to do something similar, and hopefully retain my eyesight and fingers in the meantime. I ordered a few thousand rounds of blanks to get started. I only really wanted them to test the guns but there were a lot of them and each breech of every cylinder had to be tested. Along with the boxes of rounds, I ordered in a thick sheet of Perspex, as thick as I could get it, along with some metal mesh-lined gloves that were suitable for top chefs working with sharp knives (I figured if a sharp blade couldn't penetrate through then a mini explosion might also find it more difficult). As well as the mesh gloves I had another pair of gloves that had carbon fibre armour. It would prove difficult having to work with them on but I was already taking enough chances and I had grown quite fond of my digits. I had two sets of safety glasses, one pair of wrap-around goggles and another pair that were my grandad's and looked as though they had come straight from Doc Brown in Back To The Future. The Perspex was held up with a vice so there was me, two pairs of gloves, two pairs of goggles, arms covered, and behind Perspex glass that was 10mm thick. Safe as 'ouses.

The plan with the ammunition was this. Prise out the tips at the end of the blanks, pour out the gunpowder, pull out the plastic insert that was inside each blank (which they put in to get away with using less gunpowder), shape it and cut, if necessary, then file. I tell you now, there is something very unnerving about prising open a blank. It isn't for the faint-hearted.

After the first one was done, I would move onto the next. I quickly moved onto the Henry Ford factory setup again. I'd have loads lined up ready to have the tips pulled out, then I'd fill the dish with gunpowder, pull out the plastic inserts one after the other, then I'd shape them all in one hit.

For the bullets I bought slugs on eBay. They sell them for air guns but over in America they do things bigger and better so they have air guns that can fire up to .50 calibre – .50 fucking calibre for an air rifle?! That is a lot of weight for an air gun, but if you have the power behind it then why not? I'd get the slugs and have to shave them down, which I did by placing them in my drill, then with each one they would be spun over a file or sand paper until they were the exact size I wanted. Once that process was finished the shells would be filled back up with gunpowder again after I'd removed any tiny pieces of plastic. I'd use a piece of paper that I shaped like a cone; the same way my nan used to with the icing sugar for her cake-making. Once each shell was full, I'd press the slug into each shell casing using a tiny vice. Then after that, a quick wipe down and they were done: 9mm, .38 & .44 hollow points, ready for action.

The operation went great but there were hurdles along the way. With the .44s the old hammers needed to be shaved to remove the old rim-fire contact point. The flat spot on the hammers then needed to have a centre-fire firing pin added. The hammers were big so the pins had to be welded. At first, I thought I could do it with a 9-inch nail and cut it down and shape it to size. Being that I wasn't a competent welder, I had to call in extra help which is definitely something I didn't want to do. Remember, the only time that three people can keep a secret is when two of them are dead. But I could trust this person. I had welded before on some car panels but this was different, it was minute, precision work. My partner-in-crime used the nail, but it had got so hot that it flopped down like a wet jelly on a mattress. In the end it was decided that drill bits would be the best thing to use. They were solid, extremely hard-wearing and would last years. They worked perfectly and were already set to the exact thickness you needed.

Occasionally the cylinders needed to be shaved by 1mm or so because on the pin-fire models there is no room between the cylinder and the frame, leaving no room for the base of the centre-fire shells to sit snug between cylinder and frame.

The other hurdle was the soldering on the semi-autos, sometimes it would hold solid and other times it wouldn't so further action had to be taken. It can prove to be very difficult working with two different metals that have different melting points but I got there in the end. After all, I had to make it work. I had invested a lot of money into this operation.

For the other revolvers (the blank firers and CO_2 pellet guns) all I had to do was get hold of a load of brass and steel sleeves. These were .38 of an inch thick on the outside and .22 of an inch thick on the inside. You could slot the .22 calibre rounds straight into them with tiny rubber rings on the end to stop them slipping straight through, and once the off-set firing pin and heavier duty spring I mentioned earlier was fitted to the hammers, they were good to go.

Finally, they were complete. It took a very long time but I had an arsenal fit for a small army and felt like I was about to enter WW3. They looked fucking cool. And with help I had done that. I had completed the whole thing in a haze, working obsessively until my fingers bled. I was on a mission and couldn't stop. I was like a thing possessed and I wouldn't stop until it was done. It's like I was on some kind of drug that only wore off when everything was complete and the operation was finished.

I felt then that I probably needed some help. I didn't have anything to slow my brain down and this was getting out of hand. It was my superpower but it was going to be getting me into serious trouble if I wasn't careful. If the police stumbled in now, I would be looking at a long time in the slammer. I needed to get rid of them. I tested a few to begin with and after that I didn't even bother. I knew they would work unless one of the rounds were faulty but I never heard anything back. What were these guys going to do? Go back to the guy who'd sold them a live-firing weapon with their money-back guarantee? What you gonna do? Shoot me? You can't, mate; your gun doesn't work…

It turns out guns are a hard sell, and you have to be extremely careful who you start talking to about them. Almost every guy wants one, and some girls, but nobody wants to do the time that comes with them. Plus, you don't want them getting into the wrong hands. Here's me talking about morals and ethics, then producing enough firepower to invade a small colony. Needless to say – they sold. It was slow at first then whoever I sold to obviously had started wagging their tongues. Everybody had broken the first rule of Fight Club. Most of them went to collectors, none of them went to the wannabe plastic gangsters and none went onto the street. You'd be surprised at how many collectors there actually are and how many innocent looking garages, spare rooms and mancaves contain these types of collections.

I have found it to be true that the loudest one in the room is in fact usually the tamest. It's the quiet ones that you really need to look out for, the ones that blend in quietly within society. They are the real gangsters. None of this Ronnie and Reggie Kray or John Gotti bullshit. That's not to say that they weren't gangsters, but they weren't very clever. A good gangster is not a celebrity. The last thing he wants to do is be known. It isn't good for business. Gotti brought down the Italian-American Mafia with his antics and the Krays did the same with the East End of London in Britain. They got the fame that they desired, then infamously spent the rest of their lives behind bars – taking their whole crews with them.

Don't advertise what you do, involve as few people as possible and keep your mouth shut. Everybody fucks these three golden rules up. People everywhere, especially in England, but also abroad, they seem to think that if you buy yourself a gold chain, some tattoos and an ounce of weed or coke then you automatically become a 'gungsta'. Owning a second-hand Audi or BMW with 100+ thousand miles on it with a cheap private plate, alloy wheels and tinted windows does not make you a gangster. It makes you a fucking idiot, a wannabe, a plastic.

I understand why people do it. To be noticed, to stand out, but also to fit in with a certain crew. The trouble is you ARE standing out and you ARE being noticed, by the same people you are trying to not get caught by in the first place. Rich house/poor car, or modest house/sensible car. Even the ones that are doing it 'right' and have legitimate businesses, they splash out to show off their riches, and it's great, but it doesn't last, most of the time it is short-lived. Make it your job, and not your lifestyle. Business is business.

Most of the people that live local to me live poor house/rich car – that doesn't make any sense to me. Drug dealers that make about as much as I did with drugs, fuck all, but drive about in something they think looks impressive – emulating their successful drug dealer heroes. All you're going to achieve is getting pulled over every five minutes, losing your stash and an expensive garage bill for the twat mobile.

Back to the armed visit.

The police had swooped and I was under questioning. They said they had been alerted because of the blank guns that I had purchased online. They wanted to know why I had bought them and what I was intending to do with them. Each one of the team was the same, early to mid-thirties, same haircuts – short, back and sides – confident and pushy and spoke as if they owned the joint. All ex-military, either army or marines. I only spoke when spoken to and tried to keep my answers to a simple yes or no, but they wanted an explanation so I had to give them something. I knew that they didn't have anything concrete, or else they would have knocked the door off its hinges and I would've been face-down in the Wilton.

I told them about my passion for weapons as a kid and of going to Spain and bringing stuff back as a hobby. I told them about my collection that was handed in to the police when I met my wife because we had a young son. I told them that I had stopped collecting once we'd got together and I had taken up collecting again now that we had split up again. I told them that I didn't know the laws had changed so drastically in the last 15 years or so and how badly it was now viewed to keep anything that even resembled a gun – let alone fires. All they kept asking about was the blank semi-automatics, they knew nothing about the blank revolvers from Germany, the antique revolvers from Britain, the gas-powered revolvers from Malaysia, or the deactivated Smith & Wesson. They asked me where the semi-autos were because they wanted to take them – they gave me some bullshit that they were illegal now and had to be seized because the laws had changed again. I told them it was a flash in the pan, that I had bought them on a whim then when I got them, I realised that I didn't want them, so I stripped them, cut them up until they were unrecognizable and disposed of them in the large scrap metal container at work – which would be somewhere up the scrap yard by now.

I could tell that a couple bought my story but I could see in one of the other guy's eyes that he knew I was talking shit. I let them know about my fear as they barged into my house and the worry in which I felt because of the street I lived in and what the neighbours would now be thinking. It was all bullshit but the adrenaline was there for sure. I offered to give them the two air rifles they already knew about that were in my bedroom standing in the wardrobe. You have to offer them something. They refused. The house was tidy, I no longer drank or took drugs so there was no paraphernalia lying about the place in my big, posh house. It had photos of my nan and grandad up on the mantelpiece next to the cherub ivory-coloured candlesticks holders. The place was clean – at first glance. They took a statement, didn't apologize and said if they needed any more information then they'd be back.

Thank fuck they didn't come a week earlier – I had 22 cannabis plants growing upstairs with ten lights, two fans and two air purifiers (I always had to have a few hustles on the go at any one particular time). I cut them down early because I'd had a visit from what looked like two plainclothes police officers in a white BMW, and the same again on another day from, again, what looked like two plain clothes police officers. Both times I just didn't answer the door. It turned out that one lot of them were

DEAN COOK

bailiffs who'd come to collect an unpaid debt from the family that lived there before – I knew this because they left a card. The others must have been the police.

At the time I was furious at the people who lived in my house previously – thinking they had just cost me £22,000+. In hindsight, they did me a massive favour. If they'd have come through the doors and smelled the weed then they'd have looked further and carried out an in-depth search. I didn't keep much at the house but there were a few bits and pieces that they could have made a big deal out of, like the 2000 rounds of ammunition that were sitting in my lock-up waiting to be distributed, or the 9mm and the .44 that was about ten feet away from them. A close call.

My next con was going to be my last and then I was going straight. The stress had started to overtake the buzz. So, just like the drugs it was nearly time to call it a day. Soon would be time for the 'pièce de résistance'.

CHAPTER 18

The Big One

The Finale

Up to now I'd had a good run. I'd started off by counterfeiting money, I obtained my first Rolex while still in my teens, defrauded the banks of England for a small fortune and conned my way into a full-time teaching position in a top private school. I'd cornered the world's gold market in Mickey Mouse sovereigns, flooded the country with more boxing gloves than the marquess of Queensberry, and buried as much treasure as Jack Sparrow. The great British public were sporting more Tiffany, Cartier and Breitling than they could shake a stick at and the auction houses were crammed full of antique furniture and more apothecary boxes than ever existed in the Victorian era. I started off small with my little biscuit tin of watches, but I dreamt big. I may have been a small boy that grew up in a small town, but I had some big ideas. I do sometimes wonder what I would have become, had a few things been right from the start, but I think I did okay with the hand that I was dealt. After all, that's all we can play, isn't it? That is, unless you're able to steal a few cards from under the table without anyone knowing. It isn't cheating, it's winning. As long as you can get to the finish line it doesn't matter how you got there. I had come so close to getting caught up to this point but there was no chance I would be going to prison. With my mind the way it is, I wouldn't last. I would be in a mental home before I knew it and scribbling all over the walls – a bit like the film 'A Beautiful Mind', with Russell Crowe. I had made a hell of a lot of money but unfortunately most of it from my previous cons had gone, I'd been frittering it away as I went along. It wasn't all a waste because in that time I had worked out everyone's bullshit.

I had lost my nan a year and a half earlier and my grandad before that, and it feels like forever. Their belongings were with me and have now been distributed between the family. The one thing I have kept is the clean towels. The last time they were washed was by my nan. Every so often I like to use one of them. When I do, as soon as it gets wet, the smell of whatever washing powder my nan used instantly transports me back to being a child at one of my sleepovers at their house. I like to go back and be that little boy, if only for a few seconds – safe, pure, loved and free. There was a cupboard full of it but now there are only two towels left – and soon they will be gone.

My desire to con came from having nothing, other than an emptiness which needed to be filled. I wanted to have things and thought by acquiring material possessions they would fill the void and end the need to be someone – better than who I was. After getting everything I never had, I realised that these things were just for show and in themselves just as empty. I've come to understand it was tranquillity that I was looking for. I've had to re-learn that I am somebody without material things.

Since giving up the sex, drugs and rock'n'roll and writing this book I have realised that I am, in fact, ADHD as fuck and I never knew it. I thought I was a bit obsessive at times but that was it. The weed didn't give me OCD at all; it just made my symptoms worse when the weed turned on me. Of course I was going to be an addict, it was inevitable that I would take a liking to alcohol, cannabis and Valium; because these are the three main things that slow your mind down. I can't believe it's taken until my forties to realise this is what I've been struggling with my whole life. It was my ex-wife who first said it to me, then a few others – but this is all still quite recent. Now it is so clear; the hyper focusing, the manic thoughts, the 3am planning, the people pleasing, the tiredness, the sleeplessness, the masking, and everything else.

My whole life has been spent chasing dopamine highs. That's why I liked to ride my roller skates, my go-kart and my BMX as fast as I could get them to go and why I built the ramps as high as I could make them. It's why I duct taped all those bags together to make a paraglider and why I very nearly jumped off a cliff. It's why I climbed the highest trees and jumped off bridges into the water fully clothed. It's why almost every car I've owned has been a pocket rocket or a v8, and why I drove everywhere at 100mph. It's why I have taken risks since my early years and have somehow been lucky enough to make it this far without dying. I've always wanted to go out in a blaze of glory rather than slowly die like a redundant flame. I never ever pictured myself getting old, couldn't see it and couldn't imagine it. Live fast and die young. In some ways I look back at the kid I used to be, knowing that I have failed his dreams. And in others I have become exactly who I was supposed to be – maybe there couldn't have been any other way.

I read somewhere that ADHD is a defence mechanism that has been learned in childhood as a necessary means of coping with what is going on around them. It all finally makes sense. I've been self-medicating since my mid-teens and sacrificing my soul to the devil for a reason. Now it has finally hit home. Fuck. At least now I know that there are things that I can do to give me happiness and peace in my mind. Now I have discovered who I am and where I need to be. Maybe I WILL burn out like that flickering flame after all. Slowly, and at peace. Maybe one day I will be able to unlock the chains of the prison in my mind – and finally escape.

Hyper focusing can be great if you can channel your thoughts into something positive without being reckless, but hyper focusing on past trauma on the other hand feels like a downward spiral into madness. Add in a sprinkle of depersonalisation, sleepless nights, panic attacks and an addiction or two, and you're in the depths of hell.

Yesterday I was referred to a therapist to discuss my attention deficit hyperactivity disorder along with everything else. I feel like they may have their work cut out for them. Doing that and getting some of this shit out are my first steps to recovery.

You've probably noticed while reading that my writing is fast paced, like a short distance race or a drug high. I've left it this way to offer you a glimpse into my world.

I wrote this book in ten days while out in Spain. I came here to feel closer to my grandparents, and it's only now I've finally realised that they are not coming back. I'm staying at the Ramada hotel, in Mazarron, Murcia, 30860. Now I can eat, and sleep.

My nan used to call me Little Boy Blue.

Are you ready for it? The big one? The pièce de résistance? The grand finale? Well, here goes…

LITTLE BOY BLUE

222

YOU'VE BEEN SCAMMED.

You see how easy that was? I sold you a story and a pack of lies and you bought it. That's exactly how a con works. You're led on and on, right up until the last moment, then bam. Your money has gone. And so has YOUR money, because you bought this book. All that shit about being a poor defenceless little boy who had to run away to his grandparents to escape. I wasn't a poor defenceless little boy. There never was a little boy. My name is Ima Fox. I am female. And I am German, not British. I came over to Britain and married my husband. We have two children, both boys, and a dog. But I got you, didn't I? The name on the book cover, the description on the back, and even a little photo. They were all part of the master plan. Did you fall for it? Or did you not? There have been a few clues and hidden messages throughout this story, starting from the contents page and throughout. Some of you will have spotted some already, and some of you haven't. And this is how scams end, abruptly, quickly. Then nothing.

Thank you for your money.

The Proceeds of Crime Act 2002 (POCA) is a UK law aimed at preventing and disrupting criminal activity by depriving criminals of the proceeds of their crimes. It primarily focuses on confiscating assets obtained through illegal activities and preventing money laundering. POCA also provides investigative powers like search and seizure warrants and allows for the freezing of assets.

The Proceeds of Crime act stops ex-criminals from writing and benefiting financially from any previous criminal activity.

Unless it is a work of 'fiction'.

www.ingramcontent.com/pod-product-compliance
Lightning Source LLC
LaVergne TN
LVHW091250080426
835510LV00007B/202